PENGUIN AFRICAN LIBRARY AP16

Edited by Ronald Segal

Nasser's Egypt

PETER MANSFIELD

PETER MANSFIELD

Nasser's Egypt

Penguin Books
BALTIMORE · MARYLAND

To my Mother and Father

Penguin Books Ltd, Harmondsworth, Middlesex, England
Penguin Books Inc., 3300 Clipper Mill Road, Baltimore 11, Md, U.S.A.
Penguin Books Pty Ltd, Ringwood, Victoria, Australia

First published simultaneously by Penguin Books and Pall Mall 1965

Copyright © Peter Mansfield 1965

Made and printed in Great Britain by C. Nicholls & Company Ltd
Set in Monotype Plantin

Contents

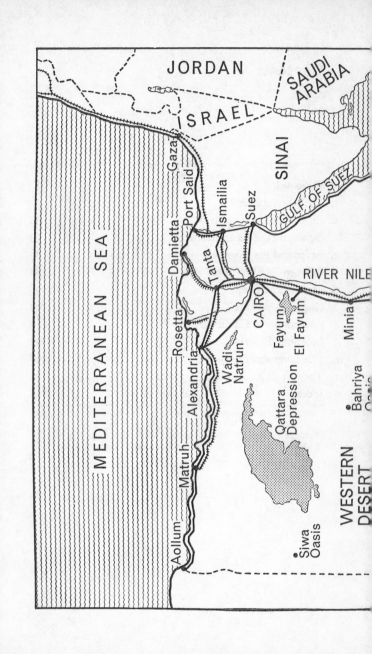

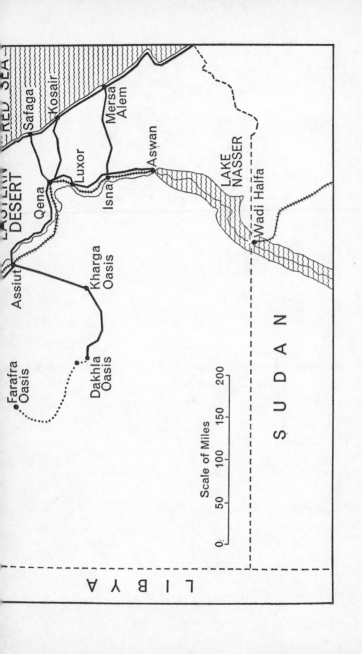

Foreword

The Egyptians are a docile and humorous people. Assassinations have had a place in their history, but generally it has been the foreigners – Syrians, Turks, Circassians, and in the modern era French, British, and Germans – who have fought across their territory while the Egyptian people stood and stared.

Bouts of Egyptian militarism – under Ramses II, or Muhammad Aly and Ibrahim Pasha in the nineteenth century – were always brief. The Egyptian Revolution, which deposed a hundred-and-fifty-year-old dynasty and destroyed the well-entrenched power of an immensely wealthy and self-confident ruling class, can claim to be the least violent in recorded history.

Yet no country in the world today arouses such strong feelings as Egypt. Gamal Abdul Nasser, who is personally responsible for the course of much of his country's modern history, is one of the most controversial national figures alive today. He is the object of admiration, love, hatred and dislike but rarely of indifference. Opinion in the economically advanced countries of the West is mostly hostile or resentful, and Nasser and 'Nasserism' are rarely given the benefit of the doubt. In Africa and Asia feelings are much more favourable, but even there Egyptian motives and intentions are frequently questioned.

Why should a small country, with few natural resources, except one great river, hold such a key position in the world? The popular image of an Egyptian is still that of a fat figure reclining in the sun and drowsily whisking away the flies. Yet 'Egyptian imperialism' and the 'threatening spread of Nasserism' are common international clichés. An explanation is required.

One factor is undoubtedly Egypt's geographical position as the West's gateway to East Africa and Asia, a position which led Bonaparte to call it 'the most important country'. But although this explains why the great powers have always wanted to control Egypt, it does not explain why they regard it as a threat to their interests.

In his *Philosophy of the Revolution* (published in 1954) Nasser remarked rather enigmatically that history was full of great roles which had never found anyone to play them and that the Middle East itself was in search of a hero. Undoubtedly he had already come to the conclusion that he and Egypt were to fulfil this role. How and to what extent they can claim to have succeeded is the subject of this book.

1 The Alien Rulers

In many ways, the history of Egypt is paradoxical. Present day Egyptians can claim to be the descendants and heirs of mankind's earliest civilized community. They also know that for seven thousand years Egypt has existed as a unified nation state. Squeezed within the narrow frontiers of the Nile Valley and Delta and surrounded by deserts, the Egyptian people have evolved through the centuries national characteristics which differentiate them sharply from their neighbours to the east, west, and south. Consequently, 'Egypt' will mean something to schoolchildren of any race and 'Egyptian' conjures up a mental picture to everyone. The paradox lies in the fact that for the last third of their history – or for nearly 2,500 years – these pioneers of civilization and nationhood have been ruled by other nationalities. Their administrative system and their armed forces have either been controlled openly or from behind the scenes by non-Egyptians. The dominant social class in the cities has been foreign or has spoken a foreign language.

In the nineteenth and early twentieth centuries Britain dominated the government, while France was the strongest influence on cultural and intellectual life, and the Greeks controlled commerce. Even Egyptian nationalists found it hard to shake off the belief that this was a natural phenomenon.

Another paradox of Egypt's history is not unconnected with the first. In ancient times the name of Egypt was linked with wealth and ease. The 'fleshpots of Egypt' was the vivid phrase used in the book of Exodus, and those living along the banks of the Nile considered themselves, and were considered by others, the most fortunate on earth. By the mid twentieth century, Egypt had come to be synonymous with a hopeless, irretrievable poverty.

In fact the two pictures of Egypt are not incompatible. It is the angle of vision that has changed. In ancient Egypt the mass of the people worked hard for little reward while a small acquisitive class of pharaohs, priests, and officials lived in splendour and ease. In modern times, princes and pashas did precisely the same but, though most of them did not know it, their position was much less secure. Egypt was no longer the only civilized state in the world. The Egyptian people did not accept their miserable lot as inevitable because the revolutions against small and selfish ruling classes had succeeded elsewhere. Eventually they found leaders among young army officers who were middle or lower middle class but were unmistakably Egyptian and Egyptian-educated.

The Nile Valley, rich and vulnerable, had become a universal symbol of exploitation, and it is not surprising that the Egyptians identified the exploiters as foreigners. While there was much truth in this, it was not wholly just. Directly and indirectly, consciously and unconsciously, foreigners had brought great benefits to Egypt. Bonaparte had awakened it from a centennial sleep. The British had immensely improved the financial, administrative and legal system. French and British engineers had added to the country's national wealth by reviving and extending the irrigation system of the Nile. Swiss, Belgians, Greeks, Italians and Maltese had opened shops and hotels and created the cosmopolitan atmosphere which helped to attract tourists, trades, and capital from the outside world. Naturally, these foreigners had not made a loss on these operations, and the greater part of their profits had left the country, but at the same time Egypt's national capital had been increased. By the early twentieth century Egypt was the most economically developed country in the Middle East or in Africa, with the exception of the Union of South Africa.

But if Egypt was prosperous, most of its people felt that its prosperity benefited others. Above all, the vast and increasing wealth of the few contrasted glaringly with the poverty of the many. It made little difference whether the living standards of the *fellahin* slightly improved, as they did at the end of the nineteenth century, or fell because the birth-rate outstripped any rising productivity, as they did between the two World Wars. In either case the gap was growing wider. And this situation was something that no foreign ruler could remedy, however well-intentioned he might be and however penetrating his analysis of Egyptian society. A genuine social revolution in Egypt could only be engineered by Egyptians, and when it came it was bound to be directed against foreign influence and those Egyptians or quasi-Egyptians who depended upon foreign power.

Egypt's revolutionaries do not have to be classified as Marxists, fascists, militarists, Trotskyists, Titoists, or anything else. Egypt's history provides their driving force and their goal. A study of Egyptian history will explain, even if it does not justify, everything that Nasser has said or done, for Nasser wants most of all to make up for the 2,500 years in which this history has been shaped by others.

The last Egyptian to display military genius on the field of battle was the Pharaoh Ramses III of the 20th Dynasty (twelfth century B.C.). After his death, the Upper and Lower Kingdom of Egypt steadily declined and disintegrated. As always, the seeds of decay had been planted much earlier. Ramses III had brought in Greeks, Libyans and Nubian mercenaries to form the backbone of his army.

A Libyan dynasty then briefly controlled the country, followed by a Nubian (or Ethiopian, as it is usually called). But for most of the two centuries following the death of Ramses III Egypt was governed by local despots in the cities of the Delta. It was under constant attack from the Assyrians, who were the rising power in the east. Irrigation works fell into disuse and trade decayed.

In the seventh century B.C. there was another brief interlude in which the Saite dynasty threw back the Assyrians and restored some of Egypt's prosperity. The Saite kings were Egyptians but they depended heavily on the Greeks to maintain their power, and in 525 B.C. the Persians, who by this time had established their own great empire, conquered Egypt without much difficulty. Two thousand years of foreign rule had begun.

The Persians were ousted by Alexander the Great in 332 B.C., and on his death in 323, when his vast empire was divided among his generals, Egypt was governed by Ptolemy and his descendants. Under the wise rule of the early Ptolemies the country prospered. Alexandria, with its library and museum, became a splendid city and the intellectual centre of the world. But the dynasty declined into vicious incompetence, until Egypt was absorbed into the growing Roman Empire by Augustus in 30 B.C.

Under the Greek Ptolemies, the Egyptians had become second-class citizens in their own country, and they were to remain such for many centuries. Under Roman rule, which was vigorous and efficient in many respects, their country became an important supplier of food to the imperial capital and a military base for the Roman armies. The Romans cleared the Red Sea of pirates and revived the trade route through it to India. But Egypt was a Roman colony in the fullest sense, living under iron military government and paying exorbitant taxes. The Greek ruling class cooperated with the colonial power and retained its privileged position.

Christianity came to Egypt in the first century A.D. with Saint Mark and spread rapidly among the mass of the people, although the Greeks and Hellenized upper class remained generally pagan. By the fourth century A.D., when Byzantium replaced Rome as the master of Egypt, four million out of six million Egyptians were Christians. The liturgy of the Egyptian Church was a Greek transliteration of the pharaonic language – Coptic – and the three million Egyptian Copts of today regard themselves as the true descendants of the ancient Egyptians.

In 640, eight years after the death of the prophet Muhammad, a small army of his followers swept down from Palestine to conquer Egypt. The Byzantine kings put up some ineffective resistance, but the Egyptian people had come to detest Byzantine rule and generally welcomed the Muslim invaders. In 706 the prefect who ruled Egypt for the Ummayad Caliphs of Damascus decreed that Arabic should replace Coptic in official documents, and although the admixture of Arab blood in Egypt was relatively small, the country soon became Arabized, Arabic-speaking and predominantly Muslim. Four thousand years of pharaonic civilization, which had already almost vanished, were succeeded by a new and more vigorous culture.

In 750 the Ummayad rulers were replaced by the Abbasids of

Baghdad, who governed until 868 when Ibn Tulun, a Turk, was able to establish an independent dynasty in Egypt. A century later the heretical Fatimids overran the country from north-west Africa. Again they did so without much difficulty, because the Egyptians were tired of being misruled by Ibn Tulun's successors. The Fatimids founded Cairo as their capital, and both architecturally and culturally the two hundred years in which they ruled Egypt were among the most splendid in the country's history.

But Fatimid power declined and the Christian Crusaders took advantage of Arab disunity to invade the Middle East. The Fatimids' ultimate treachery was to ally themselves with the Crusaders against the rising power of Salah ed-din el-Ayyoubi, the Kurdish leader of the Muslim resistance to the Christian invader. But the Ayyoubid forces defeated the Fatimids, and Saladin (as he is more generally known) eventually made himself Sultan of Egypt in 1163.

Saladin himself was a wise and far-sighted ruler, but after his death the country again fell into bloodshed and anarchy, with Kurdish mercenaries and slaves involved in a hideous succession of palace intrigues. Eventually Beybars, a man of outstanding ability, succeeded in establishing his authority in Cairo, drove out the remnants of the Crusaders and defeated the Mongol invaders from the East. Thus began the period of Mameluke rule which lasted for two hundred years in an independent Egypt and then for a further three hundred years under Ottoman suzerainty.

Mameluke means, literally, 'owned' in Arabic. For the Mamelukes were Circassians originally imported from Central Asia by the Fatimids, and the dynasty maintained itself by continually bringing in fresh recruits. If the Mamelukes had children by Egyptian women, these were not admitted into the army, and so the racial purity of the curious non-hereditary dynasty was preserved. Opinions differ as to whether the Mamelukes should be regarded as savage or civilized. In fact they were something of both. On the one hand the reigns of Mameluke sultans like Qala'un and Qait Bey reached pinnacles of artistic achievement. On the other, the ferocious cruelty with which they oppressed their subjects and feuded among themselves was exceptional even for that bloodthirsty period.

In 1517 the Ottoman Sultan Selim took Cairo, and Egypt became a province of the Ottoman empire. Beybars had installed a puppet caliph from Baghdad to legitimize Mameluke rule and his last successor was removed to Istanbul. Sultan Selim massacred many of the leading Mamelukes and then installed a system of government in Egypt which virtually guaranteed that the country would never enjoy peace or orderly administration. Authority was divided among the Sultan's representative, the Divan of Notables and twenty-four Mameluke beys, and not surprisingly a continual struggle for power ensued. Private ownership of land by the farmers had been abolished under the Mamelukes, military feudal lords whose sole interest in the land was to extort as much money as possible to support their armies. The Ottoman Sultan's representatives were also primarily concerned with squeezing taxes out of Egypt, and they farmed out the profitable business of collection to the Mamelukes, who in turn employed Copts to do the actual collecting. The whole structure bore down with increasing severity upon the miserable Egyptian farmers. The cultivated area shrank and the population declined. As the French traveller Volney wrote after visiting Egypt in 1781:

Wherever the cultivator does not enjoy the fruit of his labour, he works only by constraint and agriculture languishes. Wherever there is no security in property, there can be no industry to procure it and the arts must remain in their infancy. Wherever knowledge has no object, men will do nothing to acquire it and their minds will continue in a state of barbarism. Such is the condition of Egypt.

In 1798, Bonaparte landed near Alexandria with his expeditionary force of 40,000 men. Whether the Directory's main motive for the hazardous enterprise was to cut Britain's communications to the East, to establish a French colony in a key geographical position, or simply to get rid of Bonaparte is uncertain. Bonaparte himself was happy to go as he was already dreaming of a vast oriental empire. He found Egypt in a stricken condition with a population that had fallen from seven or eight million in Roman times to little more than two and a half million. He stayed there barely a year, although his army remained until it was forced out in 1801, and the expedition may generally be accounted a failure. But he left a legacy of unrest, and for this reason Egypt's brief Napoleonic interlude was significant.

Bonaparte defeated the Mamelukes in battle although he never crushed them completely or captured their formidable leader Murad Bey. But he destroyed their prestige and paved the way for their final extermination at the hands of Muhammad Aly nine years later. Above all, with his laws recognizing the rights of private property and inheritance in Egypt, he struck at the roots of Mameluke military feudalism and began the process of restoring centralized civil government.

Bonaparte's efforts to win over Muslim opinion were unsuccessful and may easily be ridiculed. Despite his own genuine sympathy for Islam and his policy of promoting the *Ulema* and doctors of law to responsible positions, the Egyptians never thought of the French as anything but infidels. Nevertheless, the fact that the infidels generally acted with greater mercy and justice than their own Muslim rulers did not pass unnoticed. Similarly, the French did not stay long enough in Egypt to produce any direct or lasting influence on the people through the demonstration of their advanced technical and medical knowledge, the efficiency of their administration or the work of the 120 highly talented savants who accompanied the expedition. But this was Egypt's first contact with 'progressive' Western Europe, a culture from which it had been insulated by three hundred years of Ottoman rule. The ideas were scarcely understood – still less accepted – but Egypt stirred in its sleep.

The French evacuation of Egypt in 1801 left a vacuum, because Mameluke power had been undermined without being replaced. After a period of unparalleled chaos and disorder, Muhammad Aly, a young Albanian officer who had been part of a small army sent by the Turkish Sultan to try and oust the French, established his authority and was confirmed as Pasha of Egypt by the Sultan in 1807. He and his direct descendants were to rule and – far more frequently – misrule for the next 145 years.

Muhammad Aly was ambitious, cruel, clever, and uneducated. He was the founder of modern Egypt although he had no love for Egyptians. He treacherously massacred all the leading Mamelukes and made liberal use of the sword and gallows to maintain a degree of security the country had not known for four hundred years. His ambition was to create a powerful expanded Egypt independent of Istanbul, and everything was bent to this purpose, including new economic policies which were both farsighted and foolhardy. In the early years of his rule he ordered a much needed cadastral survey of all the land in Egypt and by 1818 had settled about two million *feddans** on members of his family, senior army officers, village sheikhs and bedouin chiefs. But the greater part of the revenues accrued to the central government, and in fact he 'converted most of Egypt into a huge government farm under the direct administration of the government hierarchy'.†

The Pasha admired France and during his reign sent several hundred young Egyptians to study industry, engineering, medicine and agriculture in Paris, as well as sending a few to England. He invited French engineers to Egypt, and with their help built dams and canals and introduced perennial irrigation. He also established hospitals, with the help of French doctors, and built schools and factories which were crude and primitive but were also the first of their kind in Egypt. During his reign the growing of long staple cotton and sugar was introduced.

The ultimate purpose of all these reforms was the same – to build up strong Egyptian land and sea forces. With the aid of French officers who came to train the Egyptian army and the brilliant generalship of his son Ibrahim, he proved that the Egyptian *fellahin* could form the backbone of a formidable army, as they had last done under the early Ramses pharaohs, despite the fact that they had to be conscripted with whips. The Egyptian army conquered the Sudan and suppressed the Wahhabis in Arabia. At the Ottoman Sultan's request, Ibrahim crushed a revolt of the Greeks and later, when Muhammad Aly had quarrelled with the apprehensive Sultan, he twice routed vastly

---

*A *feddan* measures a little more than an English acre.
†Helen Anne B. Rivlin, *The Agricultural Policy of Muhammad Aly.*

superior Turkish forces. The first time, in 1832, Ibrahim was rewarded with the Pashalik of Syria; but in 1839 the British Government, fearing the collapse of the Ottoman Empire – which it regarded as essential to the balance of power in Europe – joined forces with the Turks to force Ibrahim's withdrawal behind Egypt's frontiers, and the Pasha lost forever his chance of achieving independence from the Ottoman Empire.

Muhammad Aly lived another ten years but he was a broken man with declining powers. Ibrahim died before him and he was succeeded by his grandson Abbas, a gloomy reactionary, who in his short reign of five years cancelled much of his grandfather's work of modernization. But in dismantling the armed forces he also reduced the taxes and abolished the monopolies which had financed them. In many ways the long-suffering *fellahin* were better off under Abbas than under Muhammad Aly, though this was not because of any love that the new Pasha entertained for them. Abbas was xenophobic and drove away most of the foreigners from his court, but he disliked and despised Egyptians equally.

Abbas I was succeeded in 1854 by his cheerful, cynical hard-living uncle Said, who liked foreigners as much as his nephew hated them. During his nine-year reign there was some small economic progress; the Cairo–Suez railway was built in 1858, and by a decree of 1858 the *fellahin* who had hitherto held their land by usufruct were recognized as freeholders, a step of the greatest potential significance. Said's passion was the army, and he closed all the schools which were not of direct use to it such as those teaching medicine and languages. But he was to be kindly remembered by Egyptian nationalists in later reigns for his policy of promoting Egyptian, rather than Circassian or Turkish, officers.

Said's chief claim to be recalled today, however, rests in his fatal lifelong friendship with the French engineer Ferdinand de Lesseps, who in 1854 received a concession to cut a canal through the Isthmus of Suez. This concession was not ratified by the Ottoman Sultan, who was heavily influenced against the scheme by Britain, his chief ally and protector, but a century began in which Britain and France considered that they had the right and obligation to intervene in Egyptian affairs. Despite the

Sultan's opposition, de Lesseps floated a private company, raised
£E. 8 million (mostly from France and Egypt) and began dig-
ging the canal in 1859.

Said's death in 1863 brought to the throne his nephew Ismail,
son of the great Ibrahim. After sixteen years, when Ismail 'the
Magnificent' was deposed, Egypt was loaded with debt, its
finances were controlled by foreign powers, and it had lost even
the semblance of independence.

Ismail was an ugly man of intense personal charm. His veneer
of Western culture was thin but genuine; as cruel as his grandfather, he was cruel in a more civilized way. His most quoted
remark (made in French) was: 'My country is no longer in
Africa; we are now a part of Europe.' He passionately desired all
the outward trappings of 'Westernization' – roads, railways,
street-lighting, telegraph offices – while maintaining a despotic
oriental social structure. Egypt was to be part of Europe only in
a strictly limited sense.

Ismail was a prudent and highly successful manager of his own
estates, but he lacked the capacity to do the same for Egypt. Unskilled in matters of national finance, he was too proud to seek
the right disinterested advice. When he needed money, which he
always did, he borrowed more from abroad, and as his reign
proceeded the terms on which he could borrow became ruinously
unfavourable to Egypt.

Physically, there was much to show for his extravagances; in
land and sea communications, Egypt became part of the modern
world. Ismail revived his grandfather's dynamic education policy
in more liberal form, and aiming, like his grandfather, to make
Egypt more independent of Turkey, he encouraged a relatively
free Press. He rebuilt the centre of Cairo. All went well for a
time, but soon things began to go wrong. The great boom in
Egyptian cotton caused by the American Civil War came to an
end. In 1869 Ismail spent £E. 2 million on entertaining European royalty at the opening of the Suez Canal; six years later he
was forced to stave off bankruptcy by selling his shares in the
Canal Company to the British Government for £E. 4 million. It
was the first step towards the British occupation of Egypt.

By 1876, Ismail was desperate and he announced the postponement of payment on his debts. An outcry from his foreign creditors followed, and Ismail allowed Egypt to be placed under the financial control of Britain and France. A Commission of the Debt to guard the interests of creditors was set up with British, French, Italian and Austrian representatives. The situation might yet have been saved. Some British officials in Egypt favoured the repudiation of the debts as a starting-point for reconstruction and retrenchment, but the French were adamant in rejecting this. The creditors as a whole insisted that Ismail was still holding money back and could pay more.

Desperately Ismail tried to save himself. He offered to make himself a constitutional monarch and when he had been obliged to accept a government with an Armenian Prime Minister, a British Finance Minister and a French Minister of Public Works, he made use of Egyptian nationalist feelings to force their resignation and appoint an all-Egyptian ministry headed by the liberal Sherif Pasha.

But it was too late, for the Egyptian people distrusted him – with good reason. The army bitterly resented his promotion of Turkish officers and was still smarting from the humiliation of a disastrous Abyssinian war (cf. the effect of the Palestine War seventy years later). The *fellahin*, as usual, had suffered most. With the help of the whip, the last piastre had been squeezed from them in taxation; they were poverty-stricken and heavily in debt to Greek money-lenders.

The Turkish Sultan might have been inclined to help a fellow-Muslim but he was jealous of Ismail's pretensions and aspirations to sovereignty for Egypt. Succumbing easily to British and French pressure he announced Ismail's abdication. Ismail sailed away to exile in Paris and was succeeded by his colourless, vacillating son Tewfik in June 1879.

Egyptian reformers had hopes that a new era of sound constitutional government would now begin, but they were soon disappointed. Although Sherif and the Constitutional Nationalist Party formed the government, the real power in the country belonged to the Dual Control of France and Britain, represented by advisers in the government and by the British and French Consuls-General.

Tewfik rejected a constitution submitted to him by Sherif, who resigned and was replaced by a provocatively reactionary government headed by Riaz Pasha. The inevitable result was an alliance between the Egyptian elements in the army and the liberal politicians. A successful army revolt against the hated Turkish War Minister, Osman Rifky, brought to prominence the son of a village sheikh, Colonel Ahmed Arabi, who today is regarded as the first hero of Egyptian nationalism.

Arabi was a mediocre political and military leader, but he did have eloquence and he used this gift to express the feelings of the Egyptian people, and especially the *fellahin*. The consequence of his actions may have been the British occupation of Egypt, but he was the first popular leader to demand that Egypt should no longer be dominated by foreigners.

Circumstances made him the leader of all protesting Egypt – not only of the *fellahin*, who looked naturally to the Egyptian army officers as the only outlet for their feelings, but also of the educated middle classes in the towns, who wanted an end to the despotic rule of the Khedives and had been deeply affected by the ideas of two teachers at the ancient al-Azhar University in Cairo. Jamal ed-din el-Afghani and his disciple Muhammad Abdou were both reformers, but they believed that reform had to come within the framework of Islam. It was their influence that was largely responsible for Cairo's state of intellectual ferment in the 1870s and 1880s. Meanwhile, for the brief period of his success, all the various hopes for change and reform were centred upon Colonel Arabi.

Arabi, in alliance with the Constitutionalists, held power for more than a year while the Khedive hesitated and intrigued incompetently behind the scenes. The Constitutionalists' demands that they should exercise some control over the Egyptian budget was rejected by the French and British Governments, who shortly afterwards sent their famous 'joint note' to the Khedive in which they said that they considered 'the maintenance of His Highness on the throne ... as alone able to guarantee, for the present and future, the good order and development of general prosperity in Egypt ...'.

The challenge and menace behind this note were obvious and

were accepted as such by Arabi and the nationalists. At this stage, it was the French Government, headed by the chauvinistic Gambetta, which favoured strong aggressive action, while the British were ready to compromise. But Gambetta's government soon fell, and France lost forever its power of direct political influence in Egypt.

The situation rapidly deteriorated. Arabi split with the moderate nationalists led by Sherif to concentrate on the removal of non-Egyptian officers from the army and collect petitions for the removal of the Khedive. The Turkish Sultan sent a special envoy to Egypt but in doing so showed that he did not intend to try and intervene more decisively. British and French warships were sent to Alexandria, but this failed to intimidate the Egyptians. Then, in June 1882, rioting broke out in Alexandria, and fifty Christians, including several Europeans, were killed. The rioting was put down by Arabi and the army, but the event was fatal, for it provided the justification for outside intervention. The British admiral sent an ultimatum to Arabi demanding that the building of earthworks at the entrance of Alexandria harbour should cease, as they threatened his ships. Whether the Egyptians were or were not building the earthworks is scarcely important. The admiral insisted that they were, and on 11 July 1882 bombarded Alexandria heavily.

Two months later, Gladstone's Liberal Government decided to land an expeditionary force to crush the nationalists and restore order. The Turks agreed to send 5,000 troops, but too late. France decided not to join Britain, but the European powers as a whole decided that a British occupation of Egypt was the least of all likely evils.

After a brief campaign in which the indifferently led Egyptian forces were surprised and routed, Arabi surrendered and was tried and condemned to death by a special court. By arrangement between the British and Egyptian Governments the sentence was then commuted to perpetual exile.

So Egypt's first nationalist revolution ended in failure. The mass of the people had briefly found a mouthpiece for their still uncertain aspirations. They had yet to throw up a leader with the strong nerves and cool judgement that were necessary if

Egypt was to establish its independence against formidable odds.

The political history of Egypt for the next forty years has less to do with its Khedives, who reigned as little more than puppets, than the British Consuls-General who ruled the country from behind the scenes. The first and most famous of these was Lord Cromer, who governed Egypt from 1882 to 1907. Perhaps the greatest of all British imperialist proconsuls, he combined all the faults and virtues of his breed. He was courageous, hard-working, decisive and incorruptible; he was also haughty, unimaginative and inflexible. He was absolutely certain that he knew what was best for Egypt, and he never for one moment questioned the fundamentals of his policies.

In financial terms Cromer's rule was an outstanding success. Ismail had left Egypt with a debt of nearly £E. 100 million, and after a few difficult years the debt was being serviced and the budget balanced. The financial system was centralized and simplified, a few unproductive taxes were abolished and the whip was no longer used to collect the rest.

New dams and the restoration of old ones brought immense benefits to agriculture. Cotton production rose steadily, and although cotton prices fell up to 1900, they doubled in the next ten years. Egypt enjoyed a period of unprecedented prosperity, and although prices were rising and the population growing rapidly, real *per capita* income was also increasing.

But if Egypt was prosperous it was not on the whole contented. Even in the economic sphere, where Cromer's greatest achievements lay, there were grounds for criticism. Egypt was now an agricultural country almost totally dependent on one export crop. The fantastic investment boom of the 1900s brought foreign capital pouring into the country, until by 1914 some ninety-two per cent of the capital of joint-stock companies operating in Egypt was foreign-owned, and interest liabilities to foreigners amounted to £E. 8.5 million a year. Egypt was rich but heavily in debt.

Cromer only believed in spending money for a good material return, and education and health suffered accordingly. Between 1882 and 1901 they accounted for only 1.5 per cent of the budget, and the subsequent improvement was very slight. Free education was actually abolished and school fees raised during his time in Egypt.

Cromer's economic principles were those of a nineteenth-century *laissez-faire* liberal, and – as with most of his kind – these principles fitted in neatly with his political beliefs and prejudices. Thus he was convinced that Egypt was naturally an agricultural country for which industrialization was out of the question. He was equally certain that Egyptians would be incapable of self-government for hundreds of years and that they were totally unsuited to parliamentary institutions. Not unnaturally, Egyptian nationalists have concluded that he wished to make Egypt a permanent economic colony supplying the Manchester textile industry with cotton. But it is doubtful whether Cromer himself ever saw the matter in those terms. He was a headmaster who knew what was best for his pupils.

Inevitably, after the first few years of the occupation when anything seemed preferable to what had happened before, opposition to British control steadily mounted. Britain's own position was anomalous, since it had refrained from declaring a protectorate and still regularly announced its intention of leaving. The so-called 'veiled protectorate' that resulted looked to many like a typical manifestation of British hypocrisy and so only served to increase resentment. Moreover, as Egypt became more prosperous, the gap between the rich and the poor widened. Finance and commerce were almost entirely in the hands of the Greeks, Italians, Syrians and Armenians, while the Egyptian educated classes of the towns, who were generally free to speak or write their opinions, were denied all political power. They found their outlet in the Nationalist Party led by a fiery, eloquent young lawyer called Mustapha Kamel, who had earned his place as an Egyptian nationalist hero when he died at thirty-four. The small Turco-Egyptian class of large landowners, who were now immensely wealthy, naturally disliked any signs of revolutionary upheaval.

In 1907 Cromer retired and was replaced by Sir Eldon Gorst. Of a more liberal temperament than his predecessor, Gorst tried for a time to conciliate the Khedive Abbas II – whom Cromer had humiliated and then ignored – and to encourage the creation of a moderate nationalist movement. But this merely infuriated the National Party, and since the 'moderates' were mostly Turks, Christians or members of other minorities, the result was a dangerous sharpening of sectional differences in Egypt.

Gorst died of cancer and was succeeded in 1911 by Lord Kitchener, hero of the Sudanese campaign. This masterful disciplinarian severely repressed the nationalist movement, but at the same time encouraged more liberal advances towards self-government than his predecessors had done. Under his 1913 Constitution, a Legislative Council and General Assembly were invested with limited but real powers, and there was some prospect of further reform. But then the First World War intervened, Kitchener returned to Britain, and Egypt fell under virtual military government for the duration. When Turkey entered the war on the German side, the Khedive Abbas was deposed as being too pro-Turkish and replaced by the elderly Hussein Kamel, brother of Tewfik and son of Ismail, who was given the title of Sultan. At long last, Egypt was officially declared a British protectorate. A powerful section of British opinion was demanding outright annexation; but in view of repeated past assurances that Britian would leave Egypt, such a step seemed unwise, especially at a time when Britain was condemning Germany for violating the Belgian treaty.

The 1914–18 war and the immediate post-war years brought an economic boom to Egypt. Cotton prices rose steeply and a favourable trade balance enabled the country to pay off a large part of its foreign debts. But at the same time all the earlier social and economic divisions were sharpened. While the rich became much richer and a small new profiteering class emerged, the mass of the people suffered severely. Prices tripled between 1914 and 1920, and the food shortage almost reached famine proportions.

The nationalists had been obliged to bide their time during the war years, but they had spent them in discussing and planning resistance to the British. When the war ended the powerful charismatic figure of Saad Zaghloul emerged as their leader. Zaghloul was of *fellah* origin, but had married into the Turco-Egyptian aristocracy. He had accepted the office of Minister of

Education in the time of Cromer, but from now until his death in 1927 he was to be the strongest political force in the country and the most formidable opponent of the British.

Zaghloul's request for a delegation (Wafd) to present Egypt's case in London and then at the Peace Conference in Paris was abruptly refused, and this was the signal for the so-called 1919 revolution, which through armed rebellion and strikes succeeded in paralysing the country for a short time. The revolt had been carefully planned and was directed by committees in Cairo and the provinces. But there were enough British troops in the country to quell it by force, and the country succumbed to a sullen and unrepentant quiet.

The British sent out a mission headed by Lord Milner to work out a constitution, but it was boycotted by all the Egyptian politicians. Then, after two more years of rioting and disorder during which Zaghloul and other Wafdist leaders were deported several times, Britain unilaterally declared the end of the protectorate and recognition of Egypt as an independent constitutional monarchy. But it reserved to Britain the security of communications, the defence of Egypt, and the protection of foreign nationals in Egypt and the Sudan until agreements could be concluded to cover them. This last point referred to one of the major causes of bitterness among Egyptian nationalists. The so-called 'Capitulations' had been granted originally in Ottomam times to foreign governments; they exempted foreigners from taxation and gave them the right to be tried in their own courts. They were the chief reason for the foreign control of Egyptian commercial life.

Sultan Fuad (who had succeeded his brother in 1917) became King Fuad, and Egypt acquired the trappings of an independent state. But it was not real independence. As the British High Commissioner, Lord Lloyd, himself pointed out: 'It was a qualified independence, an independence which was subjected to certain definite reservations.' What the 1922 declaration did do was restore to the family of Muhammad Aly a large part of its lost political power. The 1923 constitution vested legislative power in the King, and although it provided for a Chamber of Deputies and Senate, the King appointed two-fifths of the Senators and had the right to dissolve parliament. This right he used many times before his death in 1936.

There were now three major political forces in Egypt: the King, the Wafd, and the British, with the British still on top. In the years 1922-36 the same pattern repeated itself several times. The King would dissolve parliament and try to rule without one. When he could do so no longer, an election would be held in which the Wafdists always won a sweeping victory. The Wafd itself, however, was weakened in 1927 by the death of Zaghloul and his replacement by a lesser man, Nahas Pasha. In 1930, the strong but rather sinister independent Ismail Sidky Pasha was able to suspend the constitution and inaugurate five years of repressive government during which, with some success, he tackled the economic difficulties caused by the world slump.

Throughout this period, and in fact until 1952, the Wafd was the only political party in the country with any mass following. It included liberal intellectuals of the cities, but it also had roots deep in the countryside. Despite its left-wing fringe, however, its heart was socially conservative and it was always dominated by wealthy landowners. For this reason the Wafd never had the will or power to push through any of the major structural changes, such as land reform, that Egypt needed. It was revolutionary only in that it wanted to get rid of the British, and the ending of the occupation was the only programme on which all members of the party could agree.

Ismail Sidky, on the other hand, was a member of the small but powerful and well-knit class of Egyptian industrialists who together formed the Saadist Party in 1937 as an off-shoot of the Wafd. Between the two World Wars, and still more after 1939, the Egyptian industrial sector, from a very small beginning, grew and flourished. It was largely in the possession of a few wealthy families and highly monopolistic; much of it was controlled by the Bank Misr group founded in 1920 by Talaat Harb. The few millionaire industrialists maintained their close links with the big land and real-estate owners; the growth of Egyptian industry did not mean the emergence of a new industrial and commercial middle class so much as the strengthening and enrichment of the traditional upper class. Egyptian industry was protectionist and frankly appealed to nationalist feelings for support, but it was still heavily dominated by foreign capital (which was more French than British). Even in 1948 over sixty per cent of the capital invested in Egyptian limited companies was held by non-Egyptians.

In 1936, the threat of Mussolini's aggressive expansion in Africa brought the British and the Egyptian nationalists temporarily together. Previous attempts to achieve a permanent Anglo-Egyptian settlement had always foundered on the question of the Sudan, which was still nominally an Anglo-Egyptian condominium and which the Egyptians claimed as subject to the Egyptian crown. The 1936 agreement shelved the Sudanese question, officially ended the British occupation of Egypt and undertook to abolish the iniquitous 'Capitulations'. However, Britain retained the right to station troops in the Suez Canal Zone and fly-over rights for the Royal Air Force. The agreement provided for the British defence of Egypt against aggression in return for important Egyptian assistance in the event of war.

Without war this agreement might have satisfied both sides for some time, but all its provisions were very soon to be invoked. When fighting came to North Africa in 1940, successive Egyptian governments and the Egyptian people more than fulfilled their treaty obligations to the Allied war effort, despite the fact that sympathies were widely with the Axis and there was much doubt about the outcome of the war.

In February 1942, as Rommel was advancing into Egypt, the young King Farouk seemed about to summon Aly Maher Pasha to form a government. Aly Maher was suspected by the British of being pro-Axis and even of having passed on military secrets to the Italians. Although Egypt was officially neutral, Sir Miles Lampson, the British Ambassador, and the Commander of the British troops in Egypt surrounded Abdin Palace with tanks and demanded that Farouk call Nahas Pasha to lead the government. Farouk capitulated ignominiously, and Nahas remained in power for two years. But this fatal action, which seemed essential to the British Government at the time, ultimately destroyed the Wafd, the monarchy and the remains of British power in Egypt.

Despite its inefficiency and the constantly increasing evidence of its corruption, the Wafd remained popular at the grass roots of the country. It was still the expression of political Egypt. But outside parliament other parties and groups were gathering strength – the Communists, Ahmed Hussein's Socialist Party, Shaikh Hassan el-Banna's Muslim Brotherhood, and the clandestine Free Officers' movement in the army which was still unknown to anyone except its members. Of these extra-parliamentary groups the strongest at that time was the Muslim Brotherhood. El-Banna, the Supreme Guide of the Brotherhood until his assassination in 1949, was a gifted orator and organizer. Politically he was a radical nationalist, but he rejected all modernism in Egyptian thought and sought national renaissance in a revival of 'pure Islam'. The terrorist wing of the Brotherhood, created in the early 1940s, was responsible for many of the later political assassinations.

By 1943 the war was no longer an important political issue in Egypt, but as in the First World War inflation, shortages and the presence of foreign troops had brought wealth to a few and hardships to many. As the population rose without a corresponding increase in the cultivated area of land, rents and land values rose sharply. More and more small farmers, unable to live off their own land, were forced to work for the larger estates. By 1952, six per cent of Egypt's landowners owned sixty-five per cent of the cultivated area.

Egypt needed wise and firm government more than ever, but this was just what it did not have. King Farouk had lost the popularity he enjoyed when he ascended the throne as a boy. Now completely cynical about Egyptian political life, he was only filled with impotent hatred of the British who had humiliated him. The meaningless roundabout of Wafdist and Saadist governments was resumed. In 1946 the ageing Ismail Sidky showed on taking office that he retained his talent for repression. He came close to reaching an agreement with the British Foreign Secretary, Ernest Bevin, which would have meant the final evacuation of all British troops from Egypt by 1949; but once again the agreement foundered on the Sudanese question.

In May 1948 Britain ended its mandate over Palestine, and on its withdrawal the Jews there, with the support of the United Nations, announced the establishment of Israel. Jointly the armies of the Arab states entered Palestine to prevent them; but after an early advance the Egyptians, badly officered and equipped, were driven back by the Israelis, until the cease-fire in January 1949. Individuals had fought bravely including some of the Muslim Brothers and two officers who were to be heard of again – Major-General Neguib and Colonel Gamal Abdul Nasser.

This humiliation was another nail in the coffin of the Muhammad Aly dynasty. Farouk who had hoped to restore his prestige through a victorious war made matters worse by divorcing his popular Egyptian wife Farida in 1948. For the last time the Wafd won a sweeping victory at the polls in 1950 and Nahas returned to power. In the countryside the Wafd enjoyed a flimsy popularity because of high cotton prices during the Korean boom, but this soon collapsed alongside the prices. In Cairo the financial scandals of the Wafd – involving the beautiful Madame Nahas and her numerous relatives – were now common knowledge. Makram Ebeid, a former Wafdist Finance Minister who had quarrelled with Nahas, had compiled a 'black book' of their misdoings which was publicly circulated.

Sincere attempts by a few individual Wafdists to institute social reforms received no support from the party leaders, and Nahas returned to the one cause which might regain the party's popularity – British evacuation. In October 1951 he announced the unilateral abrogation of the Anglo-Egyptian 1936 treaty. Although Britain's Conservative Government expressed willingness to negotiate, it rejected the unilateral action outright and the struggle was on. The Wafd Party strong man and Interior Minister, Fuad Serag ed-Din, was forced to turn to the Brotherhood and the left-wing parties for his policy of harassing the British in the Canal Zone with guerrilla attacks and sabotage.

The Egyptians cut off fresh food supplies and withdrew the

labour force, which had to be replaced with African troops. The Egyptians could not defeat the 80,000-strong British force militarily, but they could make the base unserviceable and impossibly expensive to maintain. Britain's only alternative would be the reoccupation of Egypt, a course which some British politicians were prepared to visualize but which the Government did not feel itself able to afford.

British troops in the Canal Zone, in an impossible position, began to respond to the guerrilla attacks. On 25 January 1952 they surrounded the auxiliary police headquarters in Ismailia and gave the occupants one hour to surrender. The police bravely fought back until forty-three were dead.

The Egyptian reaction was directed as much against the Wafd for having uselessly thrown away the lives of the police as against the British. On the following day – Black Saturday – a large part of central Cairo was burned and looted, and about a dozen lives were lost. Serag ed-Din probably connived at the early part of the day's events, when British 'imperialist' establishments such as the Turf Club were attacked, but the rioting itself was organized by the Muslim Brotherhood and other extremist groups. The army did not intervene until the evening.

The next day the King dismissed Nahas and recalled Aly Maher, but Maher only lasted five weeks and Egypt then had four different governments in as many months; it was becoming difficult for the King to find anyone capable of forming a government. The corruption and extravagance of his court were a source of scandalous amusement to the world and of shame to most Egyptians. Any Minister who attempted to carry through even the mildest reforms was dismissed by a cynical Farouk.

But Farouk was not so cynical that he did not care whether he kept his throne. Recently he had become aware that a number of young army officers had grouped together to plot his overthrow.

2 Revolution

The King, his advisers and security police had been aware of the existence of a subversive group of army officers since some six months before the Palestine War. But they had never been able to discover the names of its leaders or details of its organization, and this was largely due to the conspiratorial genius of one man – Lieutenant-Colonel Gamal Abdul Nasser.

The man who was to engineer the overthrow of the monarchy was born on 15 January 1918 in Alexandria. His family was not Alexandrian but Upper Egyptian, or Saidi, from the small village of Beni Moor near Assiut. His father, Abdul Nasser Hussein, who was clearly above average intelligence, had obtained a primary school certificate from the Coptic School in Assiut (where there was no secondary school at the time) and this had enabled him to obtain a place in the post-office administration. At the outbreak of the First World War he was sent to Alexandria where in 1917 he married Fahima, the daughter of a moderately prosperous coal merchant, Muhammad Hammad, who was also originally from Upper Egypt. It was therefore a lower middle-class household into which their eldest son Gamal was born the following year. But the boy's grandfather was a *fellah* and his roots were deep in rural Egypt, as were those of the great majority of young officers who were later associated with him.

As a post-office official Abdul Nasser Hussein was liable to frequent transfer. In 1921 he moved with his family to Assiut and in 1923 to the poor village of Khatabta on the borders of the Delta and the desert. After attending primary school there for one year, the seven-year-old Gamal was sent to Cairo to be

33

looked after by a childless uncle, Khalil Hussein, who was an official in the Ministry of Works and a merchant and property dealer in his spare time.

Gamal attended el-Nahassin primary school near the Khan el-Khalil in old Cairo for three years. He was a withdrawn, thoughtful child who had already developed beyond his years in physique and mentality. He corresponded regularly with his parents, whom he only saw during his school holidays, and when he was eight years old his mother died after a short illness. He had been especially devoted to her and according to his friends the loss affected his character deeply. Soon afterwards his father married again.

In 1928 Gamal left el-Nahassin and for the next eight years attended secondary school first at Helwan, near Cairo, then at Ras el-Tin in Alexandria, and finally, when his father was nominated to a post in the capital, at el-Nahda School in Cairo. They were years of political ferment – on the surface when the Wafd was in power and below it, from 1930 to 1935, when the constitution was abolished and the country ruled by royal decree. The young Gamal threw himself into political activities with such enthusiasm that towards the end of his time at school he was attending scarcely any of his classes. However, he found time to read voraciously the writings of Egyptian nineteenth-century political and religious reformers such as Mustapha Kamel and Muhammad Abdou. He also devoured Rousseau, Voltaire, Hugo, Dickens and the lives of Julius Caesar, Alexander, Napoleon, and Gandhi.

At first he was attracted to the Wafd, which still seemed to be the effective expression of political and nationalist Egypt. But he was soon disillusioned. The Wafdist leaders had become self-seeking and corrupt since the great days of Saad Zaghloul and in any case were uninterested in the political enthusiasms of Egyptian youth. He then turned to Ahmed Hussein's 'Misr-el-Fatat' Socialist Party, whose green-shirted followers modelled themselves on the fascist movements of the 1930s. It is not known whether he actually joined the party, and although he approved of many of its aims he soon came to feel that Hussein was not the kind of leader Egypt needed. Frustrated and disillusioned, he was now almost in a state of despair. In 1935, he wrote to his friend Hassan el-Nashar:

Where is dignity? Where is nationalism? Where is what one can call the activity of youth? It has all disappeared and the nation lies asleep like the inhabitants of a cave. Who can wake them up, these miserable creatures who are not even aware of their own condition?

The students of el-Nahda school were doing their best to wake up the sleepers. In 1935 and 1936 Gamal was involved in several student demonstrations which led to violent clashes with the Egyptian and British police, and in one of them he was grazed on the forehead by a revolver bullet. Then in 1936 came the conclusion of the Anglo-Egyptian treaty which was well-received by the Wafdist politicians but detestable to ardently nationalist Egyptian youth. However, one side result of the treaty was to make possible the military revolution sixteen years later. The Egyptian army was now theoretically an ally of the British, and so Britain was anxious to improve it; at the same time, the Wafd badly needed to gain popularity. For the first time the Military Academy was opened to young men who came from classes other than the land-owning aristocracy.

Not only Gamal Abdul Nasser but Abdul Hakim Amer, Abdul Latif el-Baghdadi, Anwar el-Sadat, Gamal and Salah Salem, Hussein Shafei, Hassan Ibrahim, Zakariya Muhieddin and Kamal el-Din Hussein, who all played prominent roles in the revolution and in the government afterwards, were able to become officers as a result of this change of policy. In fact, among prominent members of the revolutionary regime only Aly Sabry, his brother Zulficar, and Sarwat Okasha came from upper middle-class or aristocratic families.

Gamal failed at his first attempt to enter the Military Academy in 1936, probably because of his record as a political agitator. For six months he half-heartedly studied law at Cairo University, and then in March 1937 he tried again and was admitted to the Military Academy. Despairing of Egypt's politicians he had turned to the only other way in which he could work for the restitution of the country. He was not attracted to military life as such but saw it as the only means to the goal he had already set himself as a schoolboy – ridding Egypt of British power and the rule of a corrupt pasha class.

Many years had to pass before this could be achieved. In July 1938 he graduated from the Academy with the rank of second lieutenant and was posted to Mankabad near Assiut, the principal military centre of Upper Egypt, where there were also some British officers of the military mission. At the Military Academy Gamal had begun his friendship with Abdul Hakim Amer, a friendship which survives until today when Amer is first Vice-President and Deputy Commander of the U.A.R. Armed Forces. At Mankabad he also established close ties with Anwar el-Sadat and Zakariya Muhieddin (now both Vice-Presidents). It would be an exaggeration to say that the Free Officers' movement dates from this time, but the first seeds were planted then. Anwar el-Sadat records that the young officers resented the behaviour of their Egyptian superiors who were arrogant towards them and subservient towards the British. As they endlessly discussed the ills of Egypt, the twenty-year-old Gamal revealed himself as their natural leader through the depth and weight of his personality.

Early in 1939 second-lieutenant Gamal Abdul Nasser asked to be transferred to the Sudan – nominally an Anglo-Egyptian condominium but in fact ruled by the British who took care to isolate the Sudanese troops from the Egyptians – and there he was joined by his close friend Abdul Hakim Amer. He was promoted to lieutenant and then, in September 1942, promoted further to captain and returned to Cairo, where he was appointed instructor at the Military Academy.

In his absence from Egypt much had been happening. When the Second World War broke out the young nationalist officers' doubts about Italian imperialist ambitions in Africa were overcome by their hopes that the Italians and Germans between them would force the British to evacuate Egypt. Among politicians it was the Italophile Aly Maher Pasha whom they most admired and among army leaders General Aziz el-Masri, whom Churchill insisted that the Egyptian Government dismiss for his known pro-Axis sentiments.

With Nasser and Amer in the Sudan, the nascent revolutionary movement in the army was led by Anwar el-Sadat who by now had been posted to Cairo. Impetuous and much less methodical than either of his colleagues, Sadat had soon made contact with General Masri, now in retirement, and also with the German headquarters in Libya. The Germans were anxious to help Masri escape from Egypt and then use him for their own purposes, but several unsuccessful attempts only ended with the internment of Sadat himself in a concentration camp near Minieh.

Before this Sadat had also made contact with a movement possessing its own revolutionary programme for reforming Egypt. This was the Muslim Brotherhood which had been founded at the end of the 1920s in Ismailia by its Supreme Guide Shaikh Hassan el-Banna. Still in his middle thirties at this time and a man of electrifying eloquence, Shaikh Hassan believed that only a fundamentalist Islam could regenerate Egypt. His movement had grown and spread until there were branches throughout the Arab world. Through the years it had become increasingly political in its aims and by 1940 had established a terrorist wing. There were many of the brethren in the army including one of Sadat's closest associates, Abdul Moneim Abdul Raouf, and the Supreme Guide hoped to absorb the revolutionary movement among the officers into his own.

In February 1942 occurred the incident, already related, when King Farouk was humiliatingly obliged by Sir Miles Lampson to recall the Wafd to power. The young army officers were bitterly indignant, but since the King himself had given way there was nothing they could do. In October 1942 Rommel was decisively defeated at el-Alamein and it soon became clear that Egypt was not to be liberated with German help.

Captain Abdul Nasser, once back in Egypt, began patiently and methodically to build up a clandestine movement among the young officers. Anwar Sadat records that the organization was conducted through various committees: economic affairs; assault sections (concerned with recruiting and forming cells in the army and among student and workers' para-military organizations); security (charged with checking members' reliability); and terrorism. It was largely due to Nasser's influence that this last branch of the movement never went into action except in the attempted assassination of the hated General Sirry Amer after the Palestine War – an action which Nasser bitterly regretted immediately afterwards, as he records in the *Philosophy of the Revolution*. He had an instinctive dislike of bloodshed and believed that assassination was an ineffective revolutionary weapon.

He organized the movement in such a way that while he held all the strings in his hand, both friends and enemies were equally unaware that he was the leader. Except for himself and Amer, even those in the inner circle of the movement did not know the composition of all the cells or the details of the organization.

During these years Captain Nasser found time, apart from his duties as an instructor in the Academy and the demands of the revolutionary movement itself, for a truly astonishing amount of reading. Thanks to the patient researches of George Vaucher (*Gamal Abdel Nasser et Son Equipe*, Vol. I), we know which books he borrowed from the Military Academy Library, both when he was a student and an instructor. It is a formidable combination of history, political biography, and military strategy, for the most part in English which he could now speak and read without difficulty.

In 1944 he married Tahia Khazem, the daughter of a comfortably situated merchant of Iranian origin. Shy and retiring, she has taken little part in public life during her husband's presidency, although she began to appear more frequently during Mr Khruschev's visit to Egypt with his family in 1964. But with intelligent devotion she has provided him and their five children with a calm and contented domestic background.

On 15 May 1948 Britain relinquished its mandate over Palestine, the Jews established Israel, and the Arab States at once ordered their armies to enter Palestine. On 12 May Captain Nasser had successfully passed his staff college examination. He was promoted to the rank of Major and on 16 May left by train for Gaza with Zakariya Muhieddin and Abdul Hakim Amer.

The Palestine War was a bitter but valuable and maturing experience for the 'Free Officers', as they had now begun to call themselves. Some were killed and many were wounded, including Nasser himself who was hit by a bullet close to the heart. Several of them gave outstanding proof of personal courage but they were all united in their bitter feelings against the conduct of the war by Egypt's political and military leaders. The total strength of Egyptian forces available for the fighting was about 10,000 men. Food and medical supplies were inadequate and irregular, while the arms were outdated and, in some cases, totally worthless. Senior officers gave contradictory and meaningless orders while some showed downright cowardice. It is no wonder that many soldiers should have been impressed by the words of Colonel Ahmed Abdul Aziz, riding instructor and army hero, shortly before he was killed in August 1948: 'Remember that the real battle is in Egypt.'

From October until the Egyptian–Israeli cease-fire in January 1949, about a third of the Egyptian expeditionary force was besieged by the Israelis in the Faluga pocket twenty miles north-east of Gaza. It was here that Major Nasser made his military reputation through a counter-attack which prevented the Israelis from infiltrating and overrunning the pocket.

The war as a whole had been an unexpected and humiliating defeat for the Arabs. In Egypt the troubled atmosphere was darkened further by a series of political assassinations – which were mostly the work of the Muslim Brotherhood – and reprisals by the King's secret police. The Prime Minister, Ibrahim Abdul Hadi, suspected a relationship between the Brotherhood and the clandestine movement in the army. In May 1949 he summoned Major Nasser to question him about it, but without success. He knew of the existence of the 'Free Officers', but he was quite unaware that he was talking to the arch-conspirator himself.

The Free Officers who had survived the war began to meet again in Cairo and they formed an executive committee which, with few changes, was to become the Council of the Revolution. In 1950, Gamal Abdul Nasser was formally elected president of the committee, but this was kept a closely guarded secret.

At this time the Free Officers were aiming to move into action some time in 1954 or 1955, and meanwhile they began to distribute their famous mimeographed tracts denouncing the regime which were written by Khaled Muhieddin under Nasser's direction and distributed by hand both in the army and among civilians. The existence of the whole movement became widely known, but not the names of its leaders. Nasser was aware that when the time came for a revolution, they would need a senior officer with a well-known name who could act as their figurehead and give their movement weight and respectability both at home and abroad. They found him in the fifty-year-old Major-General Muhammad Neguib, who had fought with great courage in the Palestine War and been desperately wounded. Contact was made through Abdul Hakim Amer, who had been one of his staff officers and knew that he had come round to the view that Egypt needed a revolution. Neguib became a Free Officer and in January 1952 was formally made president; but because he was too well-known to avoid discovery as a conspirator, he was never made party to the secret organization, and he had nothing to do with the planning or execution of the army revolt when it came.

King Farouk feared and disliked his influence in the army and was enraged when, against his express opposition, Neguib was elected president of the Officers' Club committee in January 1952. The Free Officers had shown their strength inside the army and were now openly challenging the palace. They had already denounced the King's circle in one of their tracts for being involved in the traffic of defective arms to Palestine.

The Wafd had returned to power in January 1950 and begun its long-drawn-out struggle with Britain. The Free Officers gave it their enthusiastic support from behind the scenes by helping to train commandos to fight in the Canal Zone. But after Wafdist policy had led to the burning of Cairo in January 1952, it soon became clear that the civilian political regime was crumbling. Several approaches by the Free Officers to members of the Wafd, including Fuad Serag ed-Din himself, had met with no response. Meanwhile the state security police seemed to be coming close to uncovering the Free Officers' secret organization. The officers decided to bring forward the date of the revolution to March 1952, but an unexpected setback occurred when Colonel Rashed Mahanna, a flamboyant and erratic Free Officer whose troops, according to the plan, were to play an important part in the *coup*, suddenly announced that he had been transferred to Gaza and was cutting off contact with the Free Officers' committee. The revolution was put off until the summer, and this may well have ensured its success because the Free Officers were able to take over Cairo while the King and the Government were in Alexandria.

As the stifling summer grew still hotter the King acted with more and more provocative high-handedness. Determined to have his revenge on General Neguib and the mutinous officers, he tried to have Neguib posted to the frontiers or the provinces and to impose General Sirry Amer, the Free Officers' chief enemy who was detested for his part in the Palestine arms scandal, as Minister of War. The King was realistic enough to see that a successful revolution was possible and arranged for more of his personal funds to be sent to Switzerland. But at the same time he seems to have believed that the great majority of the army would remain loyal. He contemptuously refused to make concessions when his ministers counselled moderation.

On 10 July the Free Officers decided to act. One of them, Colonel Okasha, has described the event in a now famous passage in an article in *el-Tahrir*:

Gamal and Khaled (Muhieddin) came to my house and asked me, as they often did, to play Rimsky-Korsakov's 'Scheherezade'. Soon the symphony began to exert its charm. Gamal listened attentively, with dreamy eyes. At the last note, he stood up, lifted the needle off the record and said abruptly: 'We shall strike at the beginning of next month'.

The date was set for 5 August, but it had to be brought forward when the Free Officers received a warning on 20 July from Ahmed Aboul Fath, the editor of *al-Misri* who had close connexions with them, that the King had decided to force the appointment of Sirry Amer as War Minister and then proceed with the arrest of fourteen of the Free Officers. The *coup* was fixed for the night of 22–23 July.

According to the detailed plan drawn up by Nasser with the help of Amer, Kamal el-Din Hussein, and Zakariya Muhieddin, Army Headquarters in Cairo was to be occupied by the 13th battalion of infantry. Other units were to take over the airport at Almaza, the radio station, the telephone exchange and all key communications centres and then converge at Headquarters. Late on the evening of 22 July the Free Officers heard that Headquarters had been warned of the impending *coup* and were already holding a council of war. Nasser barely had time to warn Amer and one or two others, but as it turned out, it was not a fatal hitch to their plans. On the one hand, most of the units had decided on their own accord to move into action at least one hour earlier than they had been told, and on the other the senior officers at Headquarters put up no more than a token resistance. Only two private soldiers were killed in the entire operation.

The capital had fallen like a ripe mango. By the evening of 24 July Zakariya Muhieddin had taken over Alexandria, and Gamal and Salah Salem the large garrison at el-Arish in Sinai. Egypt was in the hands of the revolutionaries, but there remained one great danger – the British troops in the Canal Zone. Would they intervene to save Farouk as they had saved Tewfik in 1882? Nasser for one undoubtedly believed that they might.

There was no time to waste and the officers acted swiftly. Early on the morning of 23 July Neguib, who had taken no part in the *coup* itself, was called from his villa to become President of the Revolutionary Council. The next day Aly Maher was asked to form a government and sent to Alexandria with a list of demands from King Farouk which included the appointment of Neguib as head of the armed forces and the dismissal of all the King's court favourites. Aly Maher returned to Cairo with the King's acceptance, but the revolutionaries had no intention of allowing Farouk to stay on the throne. They were playing for time in the hope that the revolution could be carried through as smoothly as it had begun. Any violent popular outburst would have been fatal, for it could have justified foreign intervention.

Early on the morning of 26 July tanks surrounded Ras el-Tin palace. Some of the Royal Guards resisted, and there was a skirmish resulting in seven wounded. By this time the King was afraid for his life and signed the act of abdication in favour of his son Ahmed Fuad with a trembling hand. On the evening of the same day he left for Naples on his yacht the *Mahroussa* with Queen Narriman, the infant Ahmed Fuad, and 204 pieces of baggage. Theoretically, Egypt was to remain a monarchy for another eleven months, but in fact the century and a half of the Muhammad Aly dynasty had come to an end.

Though no one could be sure at the time, this was very much more than a mere *coup d'etat*. It was a true revolution that would affect, in varying degrees, all Egypt's classes and institutions and change the course of its history. It would also have a pervasive influence far beyond Egypt's borders. Yet its casualty list amounted to two men killed and seven wounded and it was not followed by any judicial massacre of the landed aristocracy or old regime politicians. This was wise as well as humane, for Egypt has benefited immeasurably from the whiteness of its revolution ever since. Much of the credit for it must go to Gamal Abdul Nasser who on several occasions dissuaded the Free Officers from the use of assassination during the years of conspiracy and, at the most crucial moment of all, swung the majority of the executive committee against the execution of King Farouk.

The Free Officers had been planning this revolt for years in secret against heavy odds. They had a clear idea of what they wanted to destroy in Egypt – the monarchy, the power of the landlords, foreign influence and the corruption of political life – and they had a vision of the kind of society they wished Egypt to become. But they had had very little time to consider the political techniques needed to make the vision a reality. A few of them, such as Abdel Moneim Abdel Raouf, were Muslim Brothers or 'radical reactionaries'. A few others, such as Khaled Muhieddin, were Marxists. But the great majority, including Nasser himself, could not be given any political label except Egyptian nationalism. If most of them had had dealings with political groups at one time or other, it was as allies not disciples.

When the Free Officers had succeeded with their *coup*, they had two alternatives before them: one was to return to their barracks in the hope that, with King Farouk out of the way, Egypt's political system would purge itself of the remaining rottenness. The other was to stay and govern themselves. It very soon became clear that the first course would lead to chaos; as long as Egypt's social system remained unchanged, the Wafd might still be able to win any free election under the 1923 constitution. But the party was hollow and discredited, and Muslim Brothers and Communists would just wait for it to crumble before trying to seize power themselves. This left the Free Officers with the second course, and the trouble here was that they had no political experience or ideology. They were forced to be completely pragmatic in their approach to government.

One of the first problems they had to face was that of General Neguib. In the early months after the Revolution he more than served the purpose that they had intended. His amiable, pipe-smoking, fatherly appearance gained confidence in the new regime both at home and abroad and helped to bring rapid diplomatic recognition. His popularity in the Sudan (his mother was Sudanese) was an important asset, since relations with the Sudan constituted one of the first foreign-policy questions confronting the revolutionaries. At home he soon became an immensely popular figure and his rapturous welcome on a tour of Wafdist strongholds in the Delta during late September showed how far the mass of the people had lost faith in the Wafd.

But Neguib's popularity with the man in the street and in the field eventually caused trouble with the military junta. He soon came to see himself as the saviour of Egypt with a popular mandate to lead the country. Moreover, he was fifty-one while the average age of the other eleven members of the Revolutionary Command Council was thirty-three. He was a major-general, while none of them held higher rank than that of lieutenant-colonel. He resented having to refer all his decisions to his young colleagues.

These difficulties might have been overcome, at least for some years, if Neguib had not been so different in outlook from the young officers. Despairing of politicians they had joined the armed forces as the best means of reaching a position from which to reform Egypt. Neguib, on the other hand, was typical of the best kind of senior regular army officer to be found anywhere. He was straightforward, honest, fundamentally humane and capable of inspiring devotion in his men, but temperamentally conservative and politically unintelligent. Politicians and 'experts' exploited his easy-going *bonhomie* to persuade him that radical policies would not work in Egypt, and he was all the more easily influenced because this corresponded with his own instincts.

However, before any serious split occurred within the military junta, it was able to go a long way towards consolidating its own power, for the politicians consistently underestimated the ability of the young officers to govern. J. and S. Lacouture in their *Egypt in Transition* have described the junta as striking out alternately against left and right. On 12 August the workers in one of Egypt's largest spinning mills at Kafr el-Dawar near Alexandria rioted and seized control of the factory. Fearing that this action might lead to workers' uprisings throughout the country, the junta promptly sent in troops to take back control of the mill, arrested some 200 workers and, after a brief court-martial, hanged two of the leading agitators (Nasser again voted for clemency, but this time the majority opposed him). General Neguib took it for granted that the revolt was Communist-inspired, but it seems just as likely that the workers believed the revolution had now made them the masters. In any case, the junta had made bitter enemies of the political left within a month after the revolution.

In September, the Revolutionary Command Council, as the junta now called itself, took what was the only important radical domestic measure of the early years of the revolution. The decree, which was hastily drafted because the Free Officers had done no more than sketch out the idea before the revolution, limited land holdings to 200 *feddans* (1 *feddan* = 1.038 acres), with an extra 100 if the owner had two or more children, and provided for the redistribution of the confiscated land to *fellahin* in lots of between two and five *feddans*. Compensation was low, but since it was made proportional to the land tax which owners had consistently evaded, it was difficult for them to complain too loudly.

The redistribution of the land only affected ten per cent of Egypt's cultivated area. In a sense it was a moderate measure since even 200 *feddans* of irrigated land in the Lower Nile Valley or Delta is still worth between £E. 100,000 and £E. 140,000. The reduction in rents was more radical, since it affected small and medium landowners also and benefited the poorer sections of the farming community. But even this was certainly not socialism – it might be compared with anti-monopoly legislation and redistributive taxation in capitalist countries – and Egyptian Marxists have criticized the reform law as being American-influenced (see, for instance, Anwar Abdel Malek's *Egypte Société Militaire*, p. 76). The significance of of the 1952 agrarian reform was that it sharply reduced, though it did not destroy, the political influence of the big landowners. It was largely because of its domination by the landowning class that the Wafd had consistently failed to carry through the reforms Egypt needed when it was in power, and this had led to its own decay and destruction.

Only one feudal lord tried to resist the agrarian reform by force, a bedouin chieftain from Upper Egypt named Adly Lamlum, and he was tried and sentenced to life imprisonment. But there was also covert opposition from the Prime Minister Aly Maher and Colonel Rashad Mahanna. Colonel Mahanna, as we have seen, had abandoned the Free Officers a few months before the *coup*, but his popularity in the army, especially the artillery, had obliged them to make him a member of the Regency Council. When the Prime Minister proposed raising the maximum land holding to 500 *feddans*, the junta forced his resignation on 7 September and replaced him with General Neguib. Colonel Mahanna himself remained installed in Abdin Palace as one of the Regents until October, when the

R.C.C. announced his dismissal. In collusion with the Muslim Brotherhood he was conspiring against the regime, accusing the junta of trying to establish a 'godless republic' and describing land reform as a 'Communist manoeuvre'. On 17 January 1953 the R.C.C. arrested him together with several other officers accused of plotting against the regime; he was tried and sentenced to life imprisonment, and this was later commuted to house arrest.

The only potential opposition to the regime among the political parties came from the Wafd. The others were small with no mass following and few resources. But the Wafd had substantial funds, a nation-wide organization and a firm belief in its natural right to govern Egypt. When the Revolution took place Nahas Pasha and Fuad Serag ed-Din were on the French Riviera and they hastened back to Cairo expecting to assume power. But the two wily old politicians were never a tactical match for Colonel Nasser and his young fellow officers. They sent General Neguib on a tour of the Delta to show the Wafdists that they no longer enjoyed popular sympathy, and on 10 September a 'law of political parties' was decreed which obliged them to declare publicly their political programmes, their internal organization and party funds to the Minister of the Interior. This was Sulaiman Hafiz, who was a bitter enemy of the Wafd and as a former Vice-President of the Supreme Court had detailed knowledge of its scandalous corruption. Within a few weeks the Wafd had split into factions and its leaders were busy accusing each other.

By January 1953 the R.C.C. felt able to announce the dissolution of all political parties and the confiscation of their funds. On 23 January General Neguib announced the formation of Egypt's new political organization, the 'National Liberation Rally', and on 10 February a Provisional Constitution was promulgated which placed supreme authority for the next three years in the hands of the leader of the Revolution (General Neguib) and the members of the military committee (the R.C.C.). From here it was only one short step to the abolition of the monarchy; the Egyptian Republic was officially proclaimed on 18 June 1953. On his own insistence, Neguib became President and Prime Minister, while Colonel Nasser contented himself with the posts of Deputy Prime Minister and Minister of the Interior.

By the early months of 1953 the young officers of the R.C.C. had begun to regret that they had ever given so much power to Neguib, while Neguib himself seems to have felt that he did not have enough. It was not so much that he had dictatorial ambitions as that after a long career in the army he could not accustom himself to having his orders questioned by a committee. In his autobiography, *Egypt's Destiny*, he discusses at some length why he did not become 'Egypt's Ataturk' in the early days of the Revolution and he concludes that the most important reason was 'the character of the Egyptian people themselves'. 'Unlike the Turks,' he wrote, 'the Egyptians are not inclined to accept authoritarian rule as a matter of course; on the contrary, we are inclined to resent authoritarianism unless it can be shown to be in our own best interests.' Whether in fact the Turks accept dictatorship more easily than the Egyptians is highly debatable. But the real reason why the General never came near to emulating the Grey Wolf of Anatolia lay in his own character. He had nothing to compare with Ataturk's vision, ferocious energy or ruthlessness. He was just too nice. Moreover, he could not deny that the Revolution he now headed had been planned and carried out by others.

In the long run he was no match for Colonel Nasser in the struggle for power. But his extreme popularity in the country was still capable of causing the young officers a lot of trouble. To Egyptian politicians and foreign diplomats he began to criticize the actions of the R.C.C. as ill-considered and impetuous. Although he officially endorsed the decision of the officers to set up a Revolutionary Tribunal in September 1953 which tried prominent figures of the old regime such as Mr and Mrs Mustapha Nahas, Fuad Serag ed-Din and Ibrahim el-Hadi, he let it be known privately that he disliked the whole affair and regarded some of the Tribunal's sentences as disastrous blunders. Increasingly Neguib came under the influence of those who told him the army should return to its barracks as soon as possible.

In September Nasser dismissed from the army Colonel Ahmed Shawky, a close friend of Neguib who had been openly critical of the R.C.C. In February 1954 he banned the Muslim Brotherhood after a violent demonstration by its student followers and closed its offices without consulting Neguib. Neguib, nominally still President of the Republic and Prime Minister, found his position intolerable and sent a letter of resignation to the R.C.C. on 23 February.

The letter was well-timed. On 12 February, after long and difficult negotiations, an Anglo-Egyptian agreement had been reached on the Sudan, to register the first positive achievement in foreign policy by the revolutionary regime. The Egyptians had accepted Sudanese independence on the basis of self-determination, hoping and expecting that the Sudanese government which emerged would want unity with Egypt. Neguib's popularity in the Sudan was their greatest asset and he was due to fly to Khartoum in a few days time to represent Egypt at the opening of the new parliament.

Nevertheless, after a stormy meeting of the R.C.C., the resignation was accepted. Salah Salem announced to the press that the Council had to break with Neguib because he 'aimed at dictatorship' and had played a double game by coming to an understanding with the opposition. Both these accusations were true in a sense, although they were misleading because it was the R.C.C. that had forced Neguib to make the choice of resigning or becoming a mere figurehead.

Neguib retired to his house in the Cairo suburbs which was promptly surrounded by armed guards. He was now virtually a prisoner but he still had powerful allies. In particular, Khaled Muhieddin was able to use his influence among the cavalry officers to stir up indignation against the R.C.C.'s apparently high-handed dismissal of Neguib. There was no real bond between this young left-wing major and General Neguib, except that like all the main political groups in the country – the Communists, Muslim Brotherhood, and the Wafd – he looked on Neguib as the last line of protection for political freedom against the R.C.C.'s creeping authoritarianism.

Nasser went to confront a hostile meeting of cavalry officers in the mess at Abbassia barracks. Exerting all his power of persuasion, he failed to appease them and finally agreed to their demands that Neguib should be restored as President with Khaled Muhieddin as Prime Minister. It was the blackest moment for him since the Revolution. But his own supporters in the army had rallied by this time, and it was soon apparent that Khaled Muhieddin only had minority support in the army. Neguib still had to be brought back because of the strong wave of sympathy for him that had been raised, but Muhieddin was sent into exile in Europe. Nasser had an especial affection for him and his rebellion had come as a personal blow, but he eventually forgave him and allowed him to return to Egypt. In 1964 indeed, Muhieddin was elected to the National Assembly and was appointed President of the board of directors of *al-Akhbar* newspapers.

Nasser became Prime Minister and President of the R.C.C.; on 27 February, President Neguib told a vast and wildly enthusiastic crowd in Goumhouriyah Square that the trouble had passed 'like a summer cloud' and that there would shortly be parliamentary elections. Among the mass of the people there was deep relief that the leaders of the Revolution were not after all going to destroy each other and that the comforting father-figure of Neguib had been restored. The politicians on both the left and right saw excitedly the prospect of power, and the Muslim Brotherhood now believed that it had a chance to capture control of the R.C.C.

They all miscalculated because they were unaware of Nasser's character or capacity. During the next few weeks he showed his supreme ability as a tactician. He used the opportunity of Neguib's absence in Khartoum to arrest some of the dissident cavalry officers together with a number of leading Communists and Muslim Brothers. He also began a systematic purge of the army and police. At the same time he gave every appearance of yielding to Neguib's authority and accepting the return to civilian parliamentary government. On 9 March he gave up the posts of Prime Minister and President of the R.C.C. to Neguib. Press censorship was abolished and Cairo newspapers, with support from the politicians, began to demand a restoration of complete political freedom.

As Nasser had calculated, Neguib now found himself in an impossible position. While he had become President through an army revolt, he was about to be responsible for restoring the discredited political system which the revolt had been carried out to destroy. On 25 March the R.C.C. passed a resolution which Nasser himself proposed, providing for the Council's dissolution and the restoration on 25 July of all political parties followed by free elections to a constituent assembly.

This time the army surged to the support of Nasser, and the Free Officers were able to organize demonstrations by the National Liberation Rally and the trade-unions against the restoration of the politicians. A general strike paralysed Cairo. Eventually, on 17 April, Neguib capitulated, Nasser again became Prime Minister, censorship was reimposed and the R.C.C. gave itself a new lease of life. The restoration of parliamentary democracy was postponed *sine die*.

Neguib's power was broken although he lingered on as President for another six months. The politicians had also lost their last chance to restore civilian government, but there remained two groups which remained unsubdued – the Muslim Brotherhood and the Communists. Of these the Communists were the weaker for they were divided into several factions and Nasser was easily able to round up and imprison their leaders. The Brotherhood, with its terrorist wing organized by Abdul Moneim Abdul Raouf, was more formidable. After the signing of the Anglo-Egyptian agreement in July, the Brothers attacked it violently as a sell-out to the imperialists. Then, on 26 October, they made a fatal mistake which gave Nasser his opportunity. After unsuccessfully attempting to assassinate Nasser at a Liberation Rally meeting in Alexandria, a poor workman accused the leaders of the Brotherhood of having instigated him. At once the police rounded up all the Muslim Brothers they could find and confiscated their stores of arms. Six of them, including two members of the Supreme Council, were hanged, while the Supreme Guide Hassan el-Hudaibi was sentenced to life imprisonment.

Although the Brotherhood retained some power and influence in other parts of the Arab world, such as Syria, it was broken for ever in Egypt.

The interrogation and trial of the Brotherhood leaders revealed a connexion between them and President Neguib. No real evidence was produced of his complicity in the assassination plot, which would have been totally uncharacteristic of the General anyway. But it was enough that he had been in contact with the Brotherhood and come under their influence. On 14 November he was removed from the Presidency and placed under house arrest in the outskirts of Cairo. Two years had passed since the Revolution, but Nasser now held complete authority.

3 Egypt and the Asian Arabs

Arab nationalism and pan-Arabism are terms that today are inevitably linked with Nasser. He is often said to be aspiring to establish an Arab empire that will stretch from the Atlantic to the Persian Gulf and have Cairo as its capital. Yet it was not very long ago that Egypt was regarded by Arab nationalists as being on the fringes of the Arab world, if not outside it altogether. Muhammad Aly and Ibrahim Pasha, in the first half of the nineteenth century, toyed with the idea of fostering an Arab nationalist movement based on Cairo, but for them it was primarily a weapon against the Turks. Some of their descendants, notably Khedive Abbas Hilmi, dreamed of a revived Arab caliphate under Egyptian temporal protection. But Arab nationalism as a political movement in the sense we know it today did not really arise until the end of the nineteenth century, and then its inspiration came from Beirut, Damascus, and the Hejaz rather than Cairo. Nationalist leaders in Egypt such as Arabi and Saad Zaghloul and writers such as Lutfi Sayid and Taha Hussein were Egyptian, not Arab, nationalists and did not claim to be anything else. At the revolution, and even for some time after, the chief foreign policy aim of the Egyptian Government was the unity of Egypt and the Sudan.

It was left to a Turkish-educated Syrian, Sati el-Husri, to point out that Egypt's role in the Arab world was bound to change. 'Nature has provided Egypt with the qualities and distinctions which oblige her to take up the task of leadership in the awakening of Arab nationalism,' he wrote in 1951. Already the seeds had been planted in the late nineteenth century when, owing to Egypt's semi-independence from Ottoman authority and despite the hidden British occupation, Arab writers and journalists had flourished more in Cairo than in any other Arab capital. By the late 1920s and 30s Cairo was already the cultural, though not yet the political, centre of the Arab world. It was producing plays, films, novels, magazines and newspapers on a scale that no other Arab capital could hope to emulate. Beirut was the only possible rival, but Lebanon was too small and its cultural life too fragmented into spheres of foreign influence for it to be a major centre of specifically Arab culture.

It was inevitable, once Egypt had established some identity of interest with the other – in the main newly – independent Arab states, that it should take a leading role among them. It was much the largest and most economically developed and it had its own established political institutions. When the Arab League was set up in 1945, Cairo became its headquarters and Egypt contributed the largest share of its budget. From the late thirties onwards Egypt played a leading part in Arab efforts to prevent the establishment of a Jewish State in Palestine, and when war broke out in Palestine it contributed much the largest single contingent of troops. Nevertheless, the young revolutionary officers were still Egyptian, not Arab, nationalists. As Nasser himself remarked: 'We were fighting in the field while our thoughts were directed towards Egypt.'

In 1952 the immediate aims of the revolutionary officers were clear: to get rid of the monarchy; eliminate foreign, especially British influence; and reform Egyptian society. For the first eighteen months after the revolution, the military junta had no Middle-Eastern policy at all. Nasser was suspicious of the League, which he regarded as a fraudulent imperialist conception, and he reduced its influence by removing from office its eloquent pan-Arabist Secretary-General, Abdul Rahman Azzam Pasha. He was not interested in the Asian Arab states at that time because of any mystical notions of uniting all the Arab-speaking peoples. Egypt was directly tied to them by a common history. 'We have suffered the same trials . . . we have been victims of the same invaders.' The Asian Arab states were therefore potential allies in getting rid of the remaining influence of these invaders. Unfortunately, the only other Arab state which had the making of a stable autonomous power, Iraq, was led by a man whom Nasser regarded as the invaders' chief ally – then Nuri Said. To make matters worse, he was a man of real stature and personality. It was this bitter rivalry with Nuri Said (which was much more than a mere clash of personalities) that was the main factor in involving Egypt deeply in the politics of Arab nationalism. Long before Nuri Said was assassinated in July 1958, there was no possibility of evading a collision. It has often been said that Iraqi-Egyptian rivalry for leadership of the Arabs is historically inevitable, but whether this is so or not the difference between Nuri and Nasser was one of outlook and principle. Briefly, Nuri believed that the Arabs had to remain allies of the West because Communism was their greatest enemy. Nasser believed that a Western alliance meant Western influence, an attitude which led inevitably to neutralism.

Matters came to a head with the Turko-Iraqi agreement of January 1955, which became known as the Baghdad Pact, linking Turkey, Iraq, Pakistan, Iran and Britain in a defensive military alliance. From then on the Arab League was bitterly divided, but the great weight of articulate Arab opinion appeared to be on Nasser's side. A conservative minority in Syria and King Hussein in Jordan would have favoured joining the Baghdad Pact but they found it impossible to carry their countries with them. In Saudi Arabia the royal family was opposed to the Baghdad Pact because it feared any increase in the power of its Hashemite enemies reigning in Iraq and Jordan.

It was from this time that Nasser began to become the hero of Arab nationalism and his picture appeared in shops, cafés and taxis from Aden to Aleppo and Tripoli. Most Arabs felt that here at last was the leader they had been waiting for, who could stand up to the imperialist powers. Some looked further ahead to see him recovering Palestine for the Arabs and restoring their ancient glories by uniting them in a single State. They were only confirmed in their views when he became the new target for criticism in the Israeli and Western Press.

If the ideological struggle with Iraq was one factor that was involving Egypt more and more deeply in the affairs of the

Arab world, another was the tension on the Israeli–Egyptian border. As we have seen, the young Colonel Nasser fighting in the Palestine war found that his thoughts were still in Egypt. In 1954–5 the last thing he wanted was to be involved in a second round with the Israelis for which he knew he was not prepared. But from Gaza, the small slice of Southern Palestine on the Mediterranean which had been left under Egyptian protection, Arabs were crossing the armistice line singly or in groups on small raiding expeditions. Usually it was to their own farms which they could see by daylight from the armistice line. In reply the Israelis developed the technique they have used everywhere against Arab infiltrations from Jordan, Syria or Gaza – hitting back with their army in much greater strength. At night a powerful Israeli column would advance to a small town or village in Arab territory, surround its army or police post, blow it up and shoot everyone inside. Throughout 1954 and early 1955 the situation worsened until the Gaza refugees, the Egyptian public and army were all demanding stronger retaliation. Criticism from the army, whose humiliation in 1948 had been one of the main causes of the overthrow of the monarchy, was something Nasser could not ignore. His answer was the *fedayeen* or commandos – trained saboteurs – usually Palestinians but sometimes Egyptians, who could penetrate deep into Israel to blow up installations. Their military effectiveness was doubtful, and although the Egyptian Government disclaimed responsibility for them, it was blamed by the whole world. They brought even stronger Israeli counter-attacks. Nevertheless, they achieved the supremely important purpose for Nasser of staving off demands for an immediate all-out war with Israel which he knew would be disastrous.

His popularity in the Arab world continued to grow. His decision to purchase Czech arms on a large scale in September 1955 and to recognize Communist China were further evidence that Egypt was no longer a Western protectorate. The supreme act of defiance came with the nationalization of the Suez Canal Company, in response to abrupt withdrawal by Britain and the United States of their promised loans for the Nile High Dam. When he told the thrilled expectant crowds at Alexandria on

26 July 1956 that the Suez Canal Company was nationalized, that Egypt would build the High Dam with the revenues of the Canal it had built but never benefited from, and that the imperialists could 'choke in their rage', he stirred a response in the heart of every under-developed nation.

In his anger with the Western powers Nasser made one tactical mistake when he threatened to imprison any of the Suez Canal employees who quitted their posts. But he soon corrected this and allowed the pilots to leave. From that moment he did not put a foot wrong, and it was the experienced statesmen of Britain and France whose nervous irritation caused them to commit one blunder after the other to the supreme folly of attacking Egypt in apparent collusion with Israel and against the opposition of nine-tenths of the rest of the world including the two super-powers, the United States and the Soviet Union.

Although the Egyptian army withdrew from Gaza and the whole of Sinai, had 2,000–3,000 men killed and taken prisoner by the Israelis, and lost large quantities of equipment, the net result of the entire Suez episode was an almost complete victory for Egypt. It had acquired complete control over the Suez Canal; it had removed the British civilian-manned military base in the Canal Zone and confiscated its immense stores; and it had sequestered all British and French property in the country. What was left of British influence in Egypt had gone forever. The only important item on the debit side was Egypt's loss of its military post at Sharm el-Shaikh guarding the entrance to the Gulf of Aqaba, so that Israeli shipping can now sail up to Elath, and reach Asia and East Africa without using the Suez Canal. The psychological importance of this is greater than its commercial value to Israel. The stationing of UNEF, the United Nations Emergency Force, in Gaza along the armistice line also brought the *fedayeen* raids to an end, but their value had always been dubious for Egypt. It has gained more from having a peaceful frontier which no longer has to be heavily guarded.

Thus it happened that Egypt lost the battle and won the war. The reputation of the Egyptian armed forces was not enhanced by the operation, although some recent accounts have shown that the first estimates were not altogether fair. In particular, Egyptian anti-aircraft units in Sinai fought bravely and effectively and suffered many casualties. But far more important than this was the absence of panic among the Egyptian civilians; in Port Said they even put up some effective resistance to British troops. So far from the population rising to depose Nasser, as the invaders had calculated, it was more united behind him than it had ever been. The government in Cairo survived, and within a few days of the Anglo-French ultimatum world opinion had so rallied behind Egypt that the British and French had to accept a cease-fire.

Nasser was more of a hero than ever in the Arab world. The old colonial powers had played their last card against him and lost. The Western economic boycott of Egypt, which the United States chose to join and so dissipated most of the credit it had gained through opposing the Suez action, did not bring Egypt to its knees. It meant increased austerity for the Egyptians, but this was not hard to bear for the great majority who had been living at subsistence level before. Above all, the boycott forced Egypt to turn more towards the Communist bloc and enhanced the prestige of the Soviet Union among the Arabs.

But the very success of Nasserism was causing anxiety in some areas of the Arab world. Pro-Egyptian feeling, aided and encouraged by ubiquitous Egyptian agents, was a threat to the generally conservative regimes that were then in power. All other Arab leaders had had to deplore the Anglo-French action publicly. But at least two of them – President Chamoun of Lebanon and Nuri Said of Iraq – undoubtedly sympathized with it, while regretting that it had been done in apparent collaboration with Israel. Their fears were increased when Soviet prestige in the Middle East rose at the expense of the West.

During 1957 anti-Egyptian forces in the Middle East began to show their hand. In Jordan King Hussein successfully carried out a *coup* against his own nationalist–Nasserist government led by Suleiman Nabulsi, which had wanted to establish diplomatic relations with the Soviet Union. In Lebanon the majority of the Christian half of the population, which is hostile to Arab nationalism anyway, followed the lead of

President Chamoun and his Foreign Minister Charles Malik in openly displaying pro-Western sympathies.

King Saud and his government, becoming increasingly apprehensive about the republican trend of Arab nationalism, sent troops to help King Hussein. Conservative forces in the Middle East were beginning to ally themselves against the common danger to their survival.

Meanwhile, the United States Government was doing its best to help them. The so-called Eisenhower Doctrine of 8 January 1957 named 'international Communism' as the greatest threat to the Middle East and promised financial aid to any government which helped to resist it. From this and subsequent behaviour, it was clear that the United States was trying to set up a pro-Western anti-Nasser front in the Middle East, and this turned out to be almost as serious a blunder as the Anglo-French invasion of Egypt. The United States was particularly concerned with Syria which Secretary of State Dulles feared was about to become a Soviet satellite. Communist influence and Soviet prestige were certainly strong in Syria, but a Communist *coup* was unlikely, because neutralism and nationalism were stronger. In any case, except for some conservative politicians who had lost their grip on the country, the Syrians were in no mood to seek help from Nuri Said or the United States. Instead they asked Nasser to form an immediate and comprehensive union of Syria and Egypt.

From then on events moved rapidly. In March King Saud was forced to relinquish his powers to his brother, Prince Feisal, after the Syrians had revealed an alleged plot by the King to assassinate Nasser and so prevent the Syrian–Egyptian union. Feisal was regarded as less pro-Western and more pro-Egyptian than his brother, the King, whom the Americans had astonishingly believed they might set up as a rival to Nasser among the Arabs. In May the dangerous division of the Lebanon caused by the Suez crisis developed into a muted civil war which simmered on throughout the summer with Syria, now part of the United Arab Republic, aiding and encouraging the nationalist rebellion against President Chamoun and his pro-Western government. It was Nuri Said's decision to help Chamoun which led to his own downfall and a victory for Egypt in Iraq. Brigadier-General Abdul Karim Kassem and his subordinate officer Colonel Abdul Salam Aref had been ordered in early July to proceed with their troops to Jordan. Almost certainly the plan was to invade Syria and destroy the union with Egypt. Instead Kassem and Aref seized power in Baghdad; Nuri Said, the King and his uncle Crown Prince Abdul Ilah, were assassinated; and an Iraqi Republic was declared.

Nasser and Nasserism were triumphant. Not only were they ruling in Syria, the vital Arab heartland, but their strongest single opponent in the Arab world and the only effective remaining instrument of pro-Western policies had fallen. It was true that the immediate consequence of the 14 July Iraqi revolution was that U.S. marines landed in Lebanon and British troops were flown into Jordan to prevent what was left of pro-Western forces in the Arab world from being swept away as well. But the marines did not keep Chamoun in power. Eventually the Lebanese settled their civil war themselves with a compromise which in fact gave the rebels most of what they wanted – a neutral and much less pro-Western foreign policy. King Hussein was still just on his throne, but the Iraqi-Jordanian Hashemite federation had been destroyed and it did not look as if Jordan would survive for long as an independent state.

Nasser was at the apogee of his prestige in the Middle East. He was the idol of the great mass of the Arab people, while everywhere his enemies were in disarray. But such admiration was not to last, and although there are still millions of Arabs outside Egypt who revere him, there are fewer who simply believe that the remedy for all their troubles would be for Nasser to become President of a United Arab States.

The reason is not far to seek. The union with Syria was the first practical test of Arab political unity, and all sorts of difficulties arose when a formerly independent Arab State began to be ruled from Cairo. Nasser himself had foreseen many of the hazards when the Syrian leaders came to Cairo to ask for an immediate merger of the two countries. He says himself that he felt at the time it would have been better to start with a loose federation for a transitional period, but that the Syrians insisted.

The Syrian initiative came mostly from the leaders of the Baath Socialist Party which had been formed in the 1940s by a merger of Akram Hourani's Socialist Party and the larger Baath (Renaissance) Party led by Michel Aflak and Salah Bitar. Its ideology, mostly expounded by Aflak, was a curious amalgam of Marxism, idealistic reformism and nineteenth-century racial nationalism. Its programme was extremely vague. It had a following in Lebanon, Syria, Jordan and Iraq (though none in Egypt) and it remained essentially an intellectual's party without any mass popular support. In Syria it had never succeeded in winning more than ten per cent of the parliamentary seats in elections, but it had acquired a strong position through winning over a number of army officers to its side, and Hourani and Bitar both held key positions in the government. Before 1958 the Syrian Baath had come to feel that Nasser shared many of their ideals and aims, and they saw in him someone with sufficient weight and standing to give them what they needed – popular support – and what they wanted – the power to rule Syria. It was here that the seeds of future trouble lay, for Nasser soon decided that he did not wish to rule Syria through them. The Baath were brushed aside, and its leaders either went into sullen exile or bitter opposition.

Syria has never been an easy country to govern, and the difficulties soon began to show themselves. 'Three-and-a-half-years of endless troubles', was Nasser's subsequent description of the union. Syria's political parties were all dissolved and replaced by the Syrian branch of the National Union. Nasser appointed two Syrian Vice-Presidents for the U.A.R., several Syrian Ministers in the Central Government, and a Syrian Executive Council, but he kept most of the executive and legislative power in his own hands. Some of the Egyptian officials who went to work in Syria were of high calibre, but many were not. Inevitably Syrians began to feel that they were in the position of junior partners to the Egyptians, whom many of them regard as less intelligent and energetic than themselves. In particular the Syrian army suffered from wounded pride, while Syrian merchants, businessmen, and landowners who have a long tradition of dynamic activity in a generally free economy watched with growing apprehension as

Egypt imposed its socialist principles upon them. The left was hostile as well as the right, for Communists in Syria were given as short a shrift by the U.A.R. Government as they had been given in Egypt. To make matters worse Syria's basically agricultural economy suffered three consecutive years of disastrous drought. The mass of the Syrian people were still Nasserist, believing in him personally as their leader; right up until the end of the union, they were ready to come out in thousands to cheer him. But the middle classes, merchants, army officers, and intellectuals were increasingly disaffected.

While the situation in Syria was deteriorating, relations with the new revolutionary government in Iraq soon belied the high hopes raised in July 1958. Before the end of the year Colonel Aref, who publicly favoured an immediate Iraqi-Egyptian union, had been arrested and sentenced under General Kassem's orders. Kassem blamed Colonel Shawaf's abortive revolt at Mosul in February 1959 on President Nasser. During 1959 Iraqi Communists strengthened their position at the expense of the Arab nationalists (led by the Iraqi Baathists) and although Kassem for nearly four years maintained a precarious balancing act by preventing either side from taking over the State, Nasser distrusted him and was convinced that Iraqi Communism was a danger to the whole Arab world. Kassem, an unstable and inordinately vain man, developed a bitter and jealous hatred of Nasser.

So it was that when a group of Syrian officers revolted on 28 September 1961, the governments of Iraq, Jordan, and Saudi Arabia did nothing to conceal their pleasure. King Hussein recognized the new regime within hours. Nasser at first contemplated intervening and even got as far as ordering Egyptian paratroops to land, but he changed his mind when all Syrian resistance to the Damascus *coup* quietly faded. A few days later he said that it was not imperative for Syria to remain part of the U.A.R. and that he would not oppose its re-entry into the United Nations or the Arab League.

It was a heavy blow for Nasser and it was now the turn of his many enemies to be triumphant. Some expected his imminent fall from power, while others forecast that Egypt would turn away from the Arab world to its 'natural' sphere of interest – Africa.

Nasser himself told the Egyptians: 'We must have the courage to admit our mistakes.' But in reviewing the events of the previous three years, he came to the conclusion that his biggest mistake was not to have been suspicious of the reactionaries – to have imagined, as he said, that they would 'give up and calm down'. In June and July 1961 a series of laws had been decreed nationalizing cotton export firms, banks and insurance companies, and either wholly or partly nationalizing 275 industrial and trading companies; reducing maximum land holdings from 200 to 100 *feddans*; and sharply increasing income tax. In a short time Egypt's economy had become highly socialized and Nasser was convinced that the Syrian revolt against the U.A.R. was simply the counter-attack of the Syrian bourgeoisie. He also believed, quite correctly, that the same class in Egypt sympathized with their Syrian counterparts and he feared that they might be encouraged to revolt as well. The sequestration of the property of more than 1,000 of Egypt's wealthiest families was aimed at ensuring that this did not happen by destroying them first as a class forever.

In one sense Egypt did turn back on itself after Syria's breakaway. As Nasser said on 29 September:

During the past three and a half years, we faced many difficulties in Syria. We faced endless troubles. Almost three-quarters of my time was spent in solving Syria's problems and overcoming its difficulties and hardships.

Before the union he had been absorbed by foreign policy, so that the break-up provided him with the first chance since the Revolution of devoting time to thinking through his ideas about Egypt's own political structure. The result was the 30,000-word National Charter of May 1962 which is the foundation stone of modern Egypt. It might be compared with the Magna Carta or the U.S. Declaration of Independence – except that it is the work of one man.

But although Nasser was concentrating on domestic affairs he did not withdraw Egypt into pensive isolation from the Arab world. Cairo's Press and radio continued throughout 1962 to exchange a withering fire with those of Damascus, Amman, Riyadh, and Baghdad. In all these capitals there were many with pro-Nasserist sympathies, but they were none of them allowed a hearing. The Saudis concentrated their attack on Egyptian social-ism, which they said was atheistic; even the Imam Ahmed of Yemen, ailing but still awe-inspiring to his subjects, contributed to the anti-Egyptian chorus with a critical poem broadcast over Sanaa Radio. But the most violent abuse emanated from Syria, where a series of highly unstable governments succeeded each other in rapid succession. Syrian spokesmen accused Nasser and Egypt of oppressing Syria with a reign of terror, as well as em-bezzling funds of the Syrian State Treasury. Akram Hourani publicly accused Nasser of having agreed with the Americans on the preservation of Israel in return for dollars.

Cairo of course replied to these attacks and because its infor-mation services are infinitely more highly developed than those of any other Arab State, its voice was louder. A special programme on the 'Voice of the Arabs' entitled *Enemies of God* poured out a steady abuse of King Saud and his family, King Hussein, and the Syrian 'reactionary separatists'. In his speech on 22 Feb-ruary 1962 commemorating the union with Syria four years earlier, Nasser pronounced the doctrine that 'unity of aim is more important than unity of ranks'. He explained that it was no use trying to unite Arab States with different social systems, since socialists could not close their ranks with reactionaries.

Nasser was fighting back but he seemed to be surrounded by enemies. In August 1962, at a meeting of the Arab League Coun-cil at Shtaura in Lebanon, the Syrians listed their complaints against Egypt in the most violent terms. Nasser withdrew his delegates from the meeting and announced that Egypt was leav-ing the Arab League, and although he had probably decided to withdraw before the meeting, because of the timing the Syrians were able to claim that they had 'wiped the floor with the Egyp-tians who could not answer their charges'.

The summer of 1962 was a depressing time for Egypt. Not only was it being attacked from all sides, but because of the tense atmosphere at home and the trial of French diplomats on spying charges, foreign tourists were staying away. Then, on 28 September, some officers led by Brigadier Abdullah el-Sallal in the Yemeni army revolted against the Imam Badr, who had just succeeded his father, seized the main towns and declared a republic. The royalist cause was not lost because Badr escaped and his uncle Emir Hassan hastily returned to Saudi Arabia from the United States to rally support among Yemeni tribesmen against the new republic. President Nasser at once decided to answer Sallal's call for help and a steady stream of Egyptian arms, equipment, and men began to arrive at the Yemeni Red-Sea port of Hodeida. The prolonged involvement in the Yemen which resulted cost Egypt heavily in men and money. It was unpopular among those of the Egyptian public who were directly affected by it and a matter of indifference to most of the rest. At least one Vice-President, Kamal el-Din Hussein, is thought to have been opposed to it. Yet there is no doubt that the significant effect of the Yemeni revolution on Egypt at that time was to raise the morale of the regime as a whole and start a revival of the country's political fortunes.

Nasser once again had the initiative, which he dislikes being without. In mounting the expeditionary force to Yemen he showed conclusively that Egypt's armed forces were the only ones in the Middle East about which Israel needed to worry, and Nasserist stock rose again among the people of Iraq, Syria, and Jordan. At the same time Nasser's leading opponents were now on the defensive. The defection to Cairo of seven of Saudi Arabia's precious officer pilots in October, and of the Commander of the Jordanian Air Force and two Jordanian pilots in November, showed that neither of the Arab Kings could rely on the loyalty of his armed forces. When Egyptian planes flying for the Yemeni republicans bombed Saudi border villages and the Saudi Prime Minister, Prince Feisal, asked U.S. planes to make a display of strength over Jeddah, Cairo radio was able to claim that the 'reactionaries' were being supported by the West.

On 9 February, an army revolt in Baghdad overthrew Kassem and, after a summary trial, shot him together with his close associates. Colonel Aref was installed as President, and from the first hours of the revolt, when Baghdad radio was playing Egyptian martial music, the new Revolutionary Command Council made clear that it was anti-Communist and wanted good relations with Cairo. An Iraqi delegation led by the new Deputy Prime Minister, Aly Saleh es-Saadi, reached Cairo on the eve of the fifth anniversary of Egypt's union with Syria. At a meeting before vast crowds, President Nasser declared that on the first day of the Iraqi revolution it was clear that Cairo and Baghdad had 'unity of aim'. Saadi said that relations between the two countries would go 'to the furthest limit'.

With the Iraqi revolt having established a militantly Arab nationalist unionist regime in Baghdad, it was only a matter of time before Syria's fragile government, unable to resist joint pressure from Baghdad and Cairo, collapsed also. Exactly one month after the Iraqi revolt, a military *coup d'état* in Damascus swept aside all the men who had been in power since the break-up of the Egyptian-Syrian union, and a National Council of the Revolutionary Command pledged itself to support 'the new movement of Arab unity'. On 11 March Syria formally withdrew the complaint lodged by the former government with the Arab League against the U.A.R., and by 14 March Iraqi and Syrian ministerial delegations were already in Cairo to discuss plans for the unity of Syria, Iraq, and Egypt.

On the face of it, the prospects for Arab political unity had not been so bright since July 1958. There were now five Arab countries – Syria, Iraq, Egypt, Algeria, and Yemen – which regarded themselves and each other as 'liberated Arab states'. But while it was generally recognized that the last two – because of their special circumstances and geographical positions – could scarcely be brought into anything except a loose federal union, the creation of a tripartite Iraqi-Syrian-Egyptian state seemed quite feasible. President Nasser now had the 'unity of aim' he had been asking for, as all three States repeated the slogan 'unity, freedom, and socialism'.

But the road to unity is filled with obstacles which are not removed by being ignored. This time the chief obstacle was almost immediately apparent. In Iraq the anti-Kassem revolt had been planned and led by the Baath socialists, and they now held all the key positions in the Iraqi State. In Syria also, although their power was not absolute, they constituted the single largest group in the government, led by Salah Bitar. In Syria it was less a matter of the Baath having led the revolt than of their being the only organized civilian group that the army could call upon in forming an effective administration. In Iraq the Egyptians recognized that the Baath had borne the brunt of the struggle against Kassem, and even in Syria, where Egypt had quarrelled with the Baath leadership, Cairo's only direct contact with Damascus during the years of secession had been through the Baath organization in Beirut. Yet President Nasser's deep suspicions of the Baath remained and were reciprocated. This was especially true of the Syrian Baath, with whom he had had direct dealings during the union. He had better hopes of getting on with the Iraqi Baathists, who were in firmer control than their Syrian counterparts and had no heritage of rancour over past relations with Egypt.

The underlying differences were soon to appear. In Syria there was support among the mass of the people as well as among some civil servants and politicians in Bitar's government for an immediate reunion with Egypt under Nasser's leadership. But this, not unnaturally, was not the Baathists' idea. A few idealistic Baathists felt a genuine doctrinal disagreement with Egypt. They demanded democratic freedoms and collective leadership. Others simply wanted to keep the power in Syria that they had now obtained. But all of them, both in Iraq and Syria, because of their belief that salvation for the Arabs could only come through the Baath Party, were soon led into using methods which were quite as totalitarian as anything in Egypt.

The first open rift occurred at the end of March. On 31 March the arrival of an Algerian delegation in Damascus led by the Defence Minister Colonel Boumadian was the occasion of tumultuous popular demonstrations in favour of Nasser and union with Egypt in Syrian towns. The Baathist-led government, feeling itself about to be overwhelmed, acted promptly. Brigadier Amin Hafez, the Baathist Defence Minister, was appointed Deputy Military Governor, police intervened to disperse the demonstrators and an eighteen-hour curfew was imposed throughout Syria. On 31 March also, the editor of *al-*

Nasser's Egypt

Ahram. Muhammad Hassanein Heykal whose influential Friday articles usually reflect President Nasser's views so well that they are regarded as unofficial U.A.R. Government policy statements, fired a broadside against the Syrian Baathists under the headline 'I Object'. He declared that the official party organ in Damascus, *al-Baath*, was treating the experience of the 1958 union as if Egypt had been responsible for all the mistakes and the Baath for none. Such an attitude, he added, did not make him optimistic about opening a new page in relations between the U.A.R. and Syria.

From then on the situation steadily deteriorated. 'Unionist' ministers in the Syrian government showed their disagreement with the Baath Party over the handling of the demonstrations and threatened to resign. They accused the Baathists of wanting to monopolize the Syrian negotiations for tripartite union with Iraq and Egypt. By 5 April an agreement had been patched up, and a delegation representing all the 'progressive unionist' forces in Syria left for Cairo. The talks were adjourned and resumed until finally, on 17 April, a federal state of Iraq, Syria, and Egypt was proclaimed. There was to be a twenty-month transitional period, during which the President would rule through a Presidency Council and a Cabinet. After that a legislature would take over, comprising a house of representatives with membership proportional to population and a senate with equal membership for each of the three States – very similar to the United States system. The delicate issue of whether political parties should be permitted was glossed over by the provision that popular organizations could be formed in member regions 'within the framework of a political front'.

The new union now existed on paper, but that was about all. The only possible president for the twenty-month transitional period of the new State was Abdul Nasser, and the Baathists in Iraq and Syria were quite unprepared to put the amount of power in his hands that this would have involved. For his part, Nasser was still ready to try and work with the Iraqi Baathists, but he knew that he could not do so with the Syrians unless they were prepared at least to share power with other progressive nationalist elements. Instead, throughout May and June, the

Syrian Baathists were steadily purging non-Baathists officers from the armed forces.

Pro-Nasserist demonstrations in Aleppo and Damascus were crushed and the leaders imprisoned. After the resignation of pro-Nasser ministers, the Baath was left virtually alone in power, and new cabinets formed in both Iraq and Syria on 11 May confirmed its control of both countries. On 17 May Heykal declared in *al-Ahram* that the U.A.R. was no longer able to cooperate with the Baath leadership in Syria or peacefully coexist with it.

Nasser himself still held his hand and refrained from attacking the Baath publicly, but the Syrians knew that he was bound to do so before long. In a last effort to preserve the fading hopes of the tripartite union, a Syrian delegation headed by the non-Baathist president of the Revolutionary Council, General Louay Atassi, visited Egypt to ask Nasser not to attack the Baath in his speech on 22 July, the anniversary of the Revolution. A few hours after the Syrians left Damascus airport on 18 July, an ill-organized pro-Nasser *coup* was attempted and crushed. General Hafez, in his role as Syria's Baathist strong man, took ruthless action against the *coup*'s leaders and by 21 July, fourteen civilians and thirteen soldiers had been executed – something unprecedented in the history of the Syrian Republic's many *coups*. Nasser denied to the Syrian delegation any direct contact with the organizers of the *coup*, but he told them that he thought they had been justified in trying to revolt. The Syrian delegation returned to Damascus having failed in its mission, and on 22 July Nasser made his long-awaited speech attacking the Baath. He described the party in Syria as a 'secessionist, inhuman and immoral regime', and he declared that 'the U.A.R. is not prepared to enter a union with the fascist Nazi prison government'. He added that there were still honourable people in the ranks of the Baath, but that the leadership had gone astray. 'To ensure unity there must be a single Arab nationalist movement.' Significantly, he revealed that he had known for at least the past three months that the Iraqi Baath had been allied with the Syrians against him. On 20 April the U.A.R. intelligence service in Alexandria had intercepted a message from the Iraqi military attaché in Damascus to Aly Saleh es-Saadi in Baghdad disclosing that the Baathists had decided to liquidate the Nasserists. Es-Saadi was the Iraqi minister who had done most during the previous months to throw Iraq's weight behind the Syrian Baathists.

The movement towards Arab unity seemed to be right back at square one now that Nasser had declared war on the Baath. Both sides accused the other of being the first to repudiate the Charter of 17 April, but it made little difference; the Charter was dead anyway. *Al-Ahram* began publishing the U.A.R.'s official text of the minutes of the unity talks among the three States. The Syrians replied that the minutes contained significant errors and omissions, and the radio and Press war continued with increasing vigour throughout the late summer and autumn.

President Nasser showed that he had had grave doubts about the Baath from the beginning of the union talks, and even graver doubts about the viability of the Union Charter. But he never explained satisfactorily why he had then agreed to it. He said that the Iraqis had told him that their circumstances were such that failure to reach a union agreement would be disastrous. He also said that he felt as long as there was a one per cent chance of success, a union should be tried. Yet these did not seem adequate reasons for involving Egypt in a project with such dubious chances of success, especially when he had said himself many times before that the first Syrian–Egyptian union had failed because it had been so ill-prepared.

The truth is probably that in 1962 Nasser simply could not refuse an offer of union from another Arab State – least of all Syria. Having himself become the symbol of Arab unity, he could not appear in any way to be repudiating it. Also, he must have been hoping all the time that non-Baathist nationalists would eventually succeed to power in Syria for he firmly believed, with some good reason, that the mass of the Syrian people were on his side.

The second failure at union – this time almost before it had begun – caused a significant shift in Nasser's thinking about the Arab world. He was now no longer prepared to jeopardize Egypt's internal stability by federating it with other unstable regimes. After Syria's secession he had concluded that 'unity of aim' must precede 'unity of ranks', only to discover that even 'unity of aim' was not enough. Now he was convinced that in each Arab State which formed part of any political union, all the progressive nationalist forces had to be merged in a single front. During the summer of 1963, he seemed to be contemplating a muster of all the unionist forces in the Arab States into some kind of inter-Arab organization that would rival the Baathists, who themselves announced the holding of a general conference of Baathists from all the Arab States. But the idea never matured, and Nasser himself put his finger on the reason when he said that he could not allow his supporters to come out into the open in the other Arab States for fear that they would be persecuted.

Nasser's and Egypt's handicaps as potential leaders of the Arab unity movement are handicaps of size, weight and strength. Any inter-Arab organization which has its headquarters and inspiration in Cairo is inevitably dominated by Egypt, and supporters of such an organization are labelled 'Nasser's stooges'. Nasser himself dislikes the word 'Nasserist', but it is universally used because it describes what people mean. Similarly, when the Charter of the tripartite union was being drafted, it was rumoured that Syria and Iraq had objected to being 'junior partners'. In fact, any arrangement which tried to give them equal status would be hopelessly artificial, and the knowledge of this made the Syrians and Iraqis more sensitive and difficult.

Egypt's paradoxical 'weakness of strength' explains why the Baathists, for all their lack of popular support and of practical achievement, were able to rival for a time Nasser's leadership of the progressive Arab unionist movement. Unlike Nasserism, the Baath were not linked with any one Arab State or individual.

The Baath's challenge, however, was short-lived. In Iraq its extreme anti-Nasserist wing, led by Aly Saleh es-Saadi, had by the autumn of 1963 made the party intensely unpopular. Believing, with good reason, that the Iraqi army was unreliable as an instrument of Baath policy, he had built up a para-military National Guard of young civilians who soon began terrorizing the public. When the Baath split between its moderate and extreme wings, the army, led by President Aref, took over power and dissolved the National Guard. The Syrian Baath, now led by

General Hafez as President of the National Revolutionary Council, just survived the shock, but in a weakened and dispirited state. Meanwhile King Hussein, seriously alarmed that the United States was supporting the Baathists as an anti-Communist force in the Middle East, had been putting out feelers towards a rapprochement with Egypt. In an interview with Heykal in Paris he expressed concern over the changing balance of power between the Arab States and Israel. He pointed out that hundreds of officers had been dismissed from the Syrian army, while the Iraqi army was busy fighting the Kurds.

It was the Israeli problem that provided the departure for Nasser's next positive move in the Arab world; on 23 December he invited the Arab Kings and Heads of State to a meeting in Cairo to discuss the River Jordan question. Like King Hussein he was very concerned with the military situation in the Middle East, but he had the additional worry of knowing that all other Arab States expected Egypt to bear the brunt of the fighting if war should break out with Israel, and war seemed a distinct possibility in 1964 as the Israelis announced their intention of turning on the taps to direct the waters of the River Jordan from the northern end of Lake Tiberias to the Negev Desert. This was a move that all the Arab states, individually and collectively, had sworn to prevent.

That Nasser's concern over the Jordan waters was genuine does not make it any less likely that he had already decided a summit conference would provide the best opportunity for rebuilding his bridges with the other Arab States. With the River Jordan and Israel as the subject of the conference, it was virtually impossible for any Arab Head of State to refuse to come. And at least as an occasion for reconciliation, the conference was a resounding success. In particular Nasser and Hussein overcame their bitter past enmity, and the Jordanian King played an active and important role at the conference. The ailing King Saud, with few of his royal powers left to him at home, could not really be said to represent Saudi Arabia, but his public reconciliation with Nasser at least opened the way to the restoration of diplomatic relations between Cairo and Riyadh and to the possibility of progress towards a settlement of the Yemeni problem. By the end of the conference, Egypt was on speaking terms again with all the Arab States and with some, more cordially than it had been for a long time. The only exception to this new warmth was Syria. Nasser had no private conversations with General Hafez as he had with all the other Kings, Presidents and Prime Ministers who attended. But this was really a success for Nasser's diplomacy, since the only Baathist at the conference found himself in a lonely minority.

The Arab Heads of State decided to meet again at Alexandria in September, and this time Saudi Arabia was represented by Prince Feisal, who stayed on for a few days after the conference for talks with Nasser. On the official level relations between Saudi Arabia and Egypt had improved, but the deep mutual suspicion remained. Feisal was still one of the most implacable and effective opponents of Nasserism in the Arab world. In November joint Saudi–Egyptian efforts to arrange a settlement of the Yemeni civil war collapsed, and in January 1965 President Sallal, with Egyptian backing, formed a new government that displayed an intransigently hostile attitude towards the royalists. Cairo and Riyadh did not actually revert to abusing each other, but relations were now no more than formally correct.

When the Yemeni revolution broke out in September 1962, it provided a way out of the slough of despond for Egypt; but if Nasser could have foreseen that one third of the entire Egyptian army would be needed for at least three years to support the republic, he would have had greater doubts about dispatching the expeditionary force. Once Egypt's prestige had become involved with the republic's survival, withdrawal became impossible. The operation was not a total loss for Egypt, because the battles in the Yemeni mountains proved invaluable experience for its troops; but it was very costly, and the spectacle of Egyptian planes bombing rebellious tribesmen into submission was not one of which Egypt could be proud. It was employing traditional imperialist methods to deal with a tribal society that it did not know or understand.

Apart from the special difficulties created by the Yemeni war, however, Egypt was able to maintain and even improve upon its new relationship with the Arab States during 1964. King

Hussein of Jordan visited Egypt four times in 1964 and again in February 1965. Even relations with Syria improved as General Hafez came to head a faction in the Baathist regime which favoured a *rapprochement* with Egypt. The series of new nationalization laws proclaimed by the Syrian government in January 1965 was cautiously, if a little smugly, approved in Cairo. Furthermore, relations with President Aref's regime in Iraq so improved that an agreement was signed in September 1964 for complete constitutional unity within two years. But although this meant in theory that Iraq and Egypt would form a single State before the end of 1966, Nasser showed no sign of regarding union as a matter of immediate urgency. Heavily involved in Egypt's internal affairs as he was, he seemed to think that Iraq should first solve such of its own pressing problems as its disaffected Kurdish minority, if the union was ever to be a reality. As he told a group of Iraqi teachers and students in Cairo in February 1965: 'We only achieved what we have done here after first ensuring our own national unity.'

This seems to express Nasser's current view on the means of attaining the ultimate goal of Arab unity. Essentially it is an extension of his 'unity of aims before unity of ranks' doctrine. Syria's secession and the abortive unity negotiations of 1963 have convinced him that if two Arab States are to unite, they must not only be pursuing similar social and economic policies, but they must each be reasonably united behind such policies. He sees no purpose in Egypt's federating with another Arab State whose government is so lacking in popular support that it is shortly afterwards swept from power. The regimes in Syria, Iraq and Yemen still have to prove that they have their peoples behind them.

Nasser's reconciliation with the Arab Kings is not inconsistent with these views on Arab unity. He no longer refers to the possibility of union with their countries except as a very distant goal. What he now seems to envisage is a revived Arab League or a loose confederation of independent Arab States (although with Cairo as the League's headquarters and Egypt as its most influential member) gradually strengthening their cultural and economic links. It is no coincidence that such a relationship is very much in Egypt's interest at this stage of its economic development, when it needs markets for its industrial products and capital from the oil-producing Arab States for further development.

Inevitably this means that some of the heady idealism has gone from the Cairo blend of Arab nationalism. Nasser is no longer the knight in shining armour slaughtering the black re-actionaries who block the road to Arab unity. He has kissed them on both cheeks. Some thoughtful young Egyptians feel dis-illusioned by this sudden change, but on the whole Egypt welcomes it.

Is Nasser then no longer the acknowledged leader of the Arab nationalist movement? In one sense he undoubtedly still is. The attitude of the Israelis is always revealing, and for them Nasser is the only Arab leader who has to be taken seriously. If an Arab–Israeli settlement ever becomes possible, it is with him that they would negotiate, and if there is another war they would turn the weight of their forces against Egypt as they did in 1956. It makes no difference that the Egyptians feel the loss of Palestine less personally than do the Jordanians or the Syrians. Nasser has undertaken the main responsibility for Arab strategy towards Israel, and there is no way to discard it even if he should want to. He knows that such abandonment might involve the very survival of his regime and of everything he has achieved in Egypt. If, for instance, Egyptian intelligence were to give him certain evidence that the Israelis were making progress with the manufacture of an atomic bomb, he might have no alternative except to make one in Egypt or to go to war. Rightly or wrongly he is convinced that the Israelis must attack one day to counter the growing military strength of the Arabs and to acquire more territory for their expanding population. The Israelis are pre-sumably aware that Nasser is still as anxious to avoid outright war with them as he was in 1955, but they must also know that this is because he is not yet sure that the Arabs could win. This is not the place to discuss the tragic complexities of the Palestine problem, but only to record that if a solution is ever to be found, it will have to be negotiated between Cairo and Tel-Aviv.

As one Jordanian intellectual remarked to the author: 'Nasser has put us Arabs on the map again'. He is the reason why all States concerned with the Middle East have to take Arab opinion into account where they largely ignored it fifteen years ago. In February 1965 it was he who took the risks involved in trying to stop West German arms supplies to Israel, so he naturally received the credit for it from the Arabs when the gamble succeeded. In that sense he has fulfilled the role of the long-awaited Arab hero. But although he is still a charismatic leader and a father-figure for millions of Arabs outside Egypt, by 1965 a new generation of young educated Arabs had come of age who, while still admiring and respecting Nasser's achievements, are more ready than their fathers to take an objective view of his and Egypt's leadership. This is not to say that they are all searching for an alternative – still less that they have found one. Most of those who had put their trust in the Baath have been sadly disillusioned. But they are more prepared to base their view of Nasser on his social and economic policies and his political ideas, and less on his romantic image as a twentieth-century Saladin. Nasserism is undergoing its most difficult test.

4 Egypt and the Maghreb

Egypt's relations with the Maghreb States of Morocco, Algeria and Tunisia are still nothing like as close or intense as with the Mashriq or Asian Arab countries. This position is changing rapidly and in many ways the two halves of the Arab world are coming closer together, but the division remains and will survive for many years. One of the reasons is simply the physical barrier of Libya. The populated centres of the Libyan Kingdom's Tripolitanian and Cyrenaican provinces are themselves divided by 300 miles of desolation around the Gulf of Sirte, so the country is in no position to act as a link between Egypt and North-West Africa. But such barriers can be overcome, and with Libya's growing population and oil wealth the means are available. Of more importance is the long separation in historical experience between the Eastern and Western Arabs. French rule has left its mark on every aspect of life in the Maghreb States – especially Algeria. Western Arab leaders, even if they are passionate Arab nationalists and have fought the French for years, seem to think and act in a French context. Morocco, Algeria and Tunisia all have closer economic and cultural ties with France than with the Eastern Arab world, and although they have all been endeavouring to 'Arabize' themselves since they gained independence, this will take at least a generation to have much noticeable effect.

The most important links between Cairo and the Maghreb have been political. Egypt had already gained its independence when the French North African States began to struggle for theirs. Maghrebi nationalist leaders such as Allal el-Fassi from Morocco, Habib Bourguiba from Tunisia and Ferhat Abbas from Algeria took refuge in Cairo, where they found willing encouragement in their struggle against French rule. From the beginning of the Algerian revolution in the Aurès mountains in

November 1954, Egypt smuggled arms to the rebels and helped train Algerian commandos. The Egyptian Revolution of 1952 was in itself an inspiration to the Algerian nationalists, and Egyptian material aid and moral support were subsequently important to them; but the French were quite wrong in supposing that without such aid the rebellion would collapse. The main French motive behind the tripartite attack on Egypt in 1956 was therefore based on a misconception.

Egypt wholeheartedly supported Tunisia's and Morocco's bid for independence, but since then its relations with these two States have fluctuated violently. An antipathy between President Bourguiba of Tunisia and President Nasser came into the open soon after Tunisia's independence in March 1956. It was partly due to Bourguiba's belief that Nasser was promoting his leading political opponent, Salah ben Youssef, who had taken refuge in Egypt, but the reasons went deeper than this. Bourguiba's philosophy of revolution was different from Nasser's. He favoured a moderate Fabian approach, a cautious advance from one prepared position to another. He was not afraid to declare himself pro-Western, and he never bothered to hide his dislike of Nasser's methods. There was also an element of jealousy. Bourguiba, a man of outstanding ability and intelligence, but also of vanity, could not help being aware that because of its small size and few resources Tunisia could never play as large a role in world affairs as Egypt. The situation was made worse by the frequent appearance of articles in Western journals contrasting the 'statesmanlike moderation' of Bourguiba with Nasser's 'extremism' and expressing the hope that emergent Africa would be Bourguibist rather than Nasserist.

Tunisia, together with Morocco, joined the Arab League in September 1958, but at the first meeting he attended, the Tunisian delegate attacked Nasser violently for trying to dominate the League.

Tunisia broke off relations with the U.A.R., and Cairo's propaganda organs redoubled their attack on Bourguiba. This situation remained almost unchanged until July 1961 when Bourguiba, exasperated by France's refusal to give up its Bizerta base, ordered the attack which resulted in heavy loss of

Tunisian lives. Nasser promptly announced 'full support for Tunisia in her battle for liberty', and Bourguiba and Nasser exchanged messages of reconciliation. From then on the situation steadily improved. For the first time Bourguiba showed a genuine concern for the Arab cause in Palestine. In December 1963 President Nasser was given a warm reception in Bizerta at celebrations to mark the withdrawal of French troops, and the following month President Bourguiba came to Cairo for the Arab summit conference called by Nasser to discuss Israel's diversion of the Jordan waters. He clearly enjoyed his acceptance in Cairo as an Arab nationalist leader and publicly pledged two battalions as Tunisia's contribution to the joint Arab Military Command that the conference decided to establish.

As soon as a minimum of good relations had been produced between Cairo and Tunis, it became apparent that the two regimes had much in common. Both are authoritarian but radical and reformist. Bourguiba is prepared to move faster with secularization than Nasser, and Nasser to proceed further with State control of industry; but in social and economic policy they are generally closer to each other than either is to any other Arab leader. But the new harmony did not last. When in April 1965 Bourguiba suggested that the Arabs should make peace with Israel as a start towards a solution of the Palestine problem he was acting in the way Nasser had always most disliked. He was breaking the new and painfully created façade of Arab unity and, worse in Nasser's eyes, was providing an opening for Western sympathizers with Israel to drive a permanent wedge between the Arab States on this issue. The breach between Cairo and Tunis seemed wider than ever.

Egypt's relations with Morocco since its independence in March 1956 have been almost exactly the converse of those with Tunisia. Like Tunisia, Morocco hesitated for two years before joining the Arab League; but, unlike Tunisia, it did not immediately withdraw. Between 1958 and 1960 Morocco was moving steadily if cautiously closer to the Eastern Arab world. President Nasser developed a strong admiration for King Muhammad V and in January 1960 invited the Moroccan monarch to join him in inaugurating the work on the High Dam. Although he had some interest in reform, King Muhammad remained in many respects a feudal monarch, and it is paradoxical that he, rather than the anti-monarchist progressive Bourguiba, should have been admired and liked by Nasser. The reason lay in Morocco's foreign policy, which with Muhammad V's approval became radical, neutralist and, if not anti-Western, at least much less pro-Western than Tunisia's. 1960 saw the formation of the so-called Casablanca bloc of radical African States – Egypt, Ghana, Guinea, Mali and Morocco – which contrasted sharply with the larger altogether French-speaking Brazzaville group of moderates. The Casablanca group actually agreed to form the nucleus of an African military high command and common market.

In return for its attitude Morocco expected, and got, Egypt's support for its claim to Mauretania. But it was not long before the fundamental incompatibility of outlook between the two regimes became clear. Once Algeria became independent in July 1962, Egypt's natural sympathy lay with this revolutionary socialist republic rather than with the Moroccan monarchy, and this was still more apparent when Ben Bella won the struggle for power among Algeria's revolutionary leaders. The Algerian F.L.N.'s open support for the Moroccan left-wing opposition party, the U.N.F.P., did not please King Hassan II, and although the young Moroccan monarch visited Algeria in March 1963 for talks with Ben Bella and the communiqué issued afterwards declared 'complete identity of views' between the two leaders, relations were already deteriorating. The Moroccan Government was turning away from the Arab world to closer ties with the French-speaking African States south of the Sahara. Algeria, which had sent representatives of its Provisional Government to meetings of the Casablanca group, was now nominally a full member, but on 29 April it asked for a postponement of the group's summit meeting which had been planned for 8 May at Marrakesh. In the end, the meeting was never held. At the African Heads of State conference in Addis Ababa at the end of May, both Nasser and Ben Bella had cordial meetings with the Mauretanian delegation. The Casablanca group had to all intents and purposes ceased to exist.

In September 1963, when violent border fighting broke out

between Algeria and Morocco, President Nasser unquestion-ingly supported Algeria. It is true that he offered to mediate, but it was on the assumption that Morocco had been guilty of aggression. The Moroccan Government bitterly rejected the Arab League's attempt at mediation also, because it considered that the League was siding with Algeria and Egypt. Morocco recalled its Ambassador from Cairo and expelled 350 Egyptian teachers, while President Nasser sent some 2,000 troops to rein-force the ill-equipped Algerian army.

King Hassan agreed to come to Cairo for the Arab summit meeting in January 1964, and although he left early the Moroc-can delegation signed the resolutions on his behalf. Morocco continued to vote with the Arabs at the United Nations, but there were no signs that it was ready to reverse its general trend away from the Arab world.

The question arises whether Morocco's relations would have developed differently if King Muhammad V had not died pre-maturely in April 1961. President Nasser admired and respected him, apparently believing that Muhammad was capable of maintaining his position as arbiter of Morocco's political life while avoiding the danger of driving the left wing into opposition to the monarchy. Certainly Muhammad was much more successful in this than his son Hassan, but he enjoyed the great advantage of being the hero and symbol of the country's inde-pendence and he never had to contend with a dynamic and revolutionary Algerian State as his neighbour.

The ink was scarcely dry on the Évian agreements before it was being widely prophesied that Egypt would resent an inde-pendent Algeria's rival claim to leadership in the Arab world and Africa. Since the death of Nuri Said there had been no Arab statesman of comparable stature to Nasser, and because his quarrel with the Iraqi leader was generally held to be caused by personal jealousy, it followed that it was only a matter of time before he fell out with Ben Bella. Not only has this not happened, but President Nasser enjoys an easier and closer relationship with President Ben Bella than with any other Arab leader. The reasons are not far to seek. Ben Bella is genuinely grateful to Nasser for his consistent support of the Algerian revolution and what the joint communiqué after Nasser's visit to Algeria in May 1964 called the 'effective contribution of the U.A.R. people towards the Algerian people in their heroic struggle against imperialism'. One nation's debt of gratitude to another may well, of course, turn to resentment. In this case, however, the Algerians, having fought and suffered long for their independence, do not feel any heavy obligation to the Arab States that helped them. Above all, President Ben Bella has none of the inferiority complex about Egypt's dominant position in the Arab world which is characteristic of many other Arab leaders. He has a political philosophy which is closely similar to Nasser's, but he has arrived at it in his own way (no one has ever thought of calling him a Nasserist). In many important respects, Algeria's circumstances and problems are different from Egypt's. Its agrarian system, for instance, is totally different, so that the principles of Egypt's land reform are inapplicable to it. There is no question of Egypt's relationship with Algeria being akin to that of a colonial power; such cannot be said for Egypt's relationship with Sudan and Syria in the past, or its relationship with Yemen today.

It would be rash to rule out altogether any chance of an end to the Egyptian–Algerian *entente*. Already there are signs of a divergence between the two countries in the tactics of African liberation. Ben Bella is essentially a militant. As he said during his visit to the Soviet Union in May 1964: 'Algeria has been turned into a training camp for those fighting the present regimes in Angola, Mozambique, South Africa and so-called Portuguese Guinea.' Egypt has not tried to compete with this attitude, although it is a member, together with Algeria and seven other African States, of the nine-member coordinating committee for African liberation set up by the Organization of African Unity. Egypt has given and will continue to give money and political support, but the groups actually struggling against the remaining colonial and racist governments in Africa would now look to Algeria for military aid and training in guerrilla warfare. There is no real evidence that President Nasser resents this; it is quite possible that he has privately agreed with President Ben Bella on this division of functions. But the possibility also cannot be excluded that Ben Bella will become the apostle of violent revolution in Africa, with Nasser favouring a more cautious approach.

Libya is the only one of the North African States over which Egypt has any direct political influence. That it is a powerful influence was forcefully demonstrated in February 1964; Nasser's speech calling for the liquidation of British and American military bases in the Middle East brought an immediate response from Libya, where a nervous government, urged on by Parliament and a vocal public opinion, felt obliged to request immediate negotiations for a revision of the base rights agreements.

Britain and the United States, which apart from the bases have immense oil interests in Libya, are anxiously wondering what will happen when the infirm and elderly King Idris dies and is succeeded by his little known and undistinguished nephew Prince Hassan Rida. Libya's national unity is new and fragile, and it has occurred to many that Egypt might be tempted to try and absorb neighbouring Cyrenaica, which has more than half the oil that has been discovered in Libya. But since it is highly improbable that Egypt would attempt to occupy Cyrenaica by force, this means that a revolutionary government would have to come to power in Benghazi and then ask for incorporation in Egypt. This is unlikely because however strong pro-Nasser sympathies may be among the Libyan younger generations in the towns, the years of independence – now buttressed by the new oil wealth – have already created powerful vested interests in Libya's survival as an independent nation state. This has certainly been the experience of Kuwait, which is a much more artificial entity than Libya. Partly in self-protection, Libya has begun increasingly to consider itself as part of the Maghreb, and in November 1964 joined Tunisia, Algeria and Morocco in the Tangier conference on the economic unity of the region. As with the Eastern Arab States, Egypt's best chance of maintaining and extending its influence in Libya is by scrupulously respecting its sovereignty.

5 Between East and West

Nasser's 'neutralism' or non-alignment between the two great power blocs is fundamental to his political outlook. This was an inevitable development of his passionate Egyptian and Arab nationalism which makes him want to rid the Middle East of all foreign influence, but it was not immediately evident when he came to power. In the early years of the revolution indeed, he was regarded as pro-American. The only important aim in the foreign policy of the young revolutionaries was to get rid of the British, and the United States seemed to show at least a benevolent understanding of their desire to make Egypt really independent. The U.S. Ambassador Jefferson Caffery established excellent relations with them. But this pro-Americanism did not last through 1954, largely because the U.S. Government (like so many other governments) misjudged its dealings with Egypt. American diplomacy helped towards the Anglo-Egyptian Suez settlement of 1959, American experts came to Egypt in increasing numbers, and development credits were raised to forty million dollars. But all this was nullified by the efforts of Mr Dulles to bring Egypt into a Middle East defence pact against the Soviet Union. When the Revolutionary Command Council refused, he turned to the idea of forming a bloc of 'northern tier' Middle East States, which eventually became known as the Baghdad Pact. Nasser was even more hostile to this because he believed that it would perpetuate Western influence in the Middle East and, since it included an Arab State – Iraq, would keep the Arab world divided. Cairo radio launched a violent offensive against the Baghdad Pact, and Nasser began to acquire his reputation of bitter hostility to the West.

The American Government felt that it was being badly repaid for its efforts to help the young Egyptian republic. The British

Government was also resentful. It was carrying out the terms of the Anglo-Egyptian agreement, it was releasing Egypt's blocked sterling balances, and it had sent a small quantity of arms. But neither Britain nor the United States had yet understood that Egypt would no longer be treated as a semi-independent Western protectorate. As Nasser remarked in an interview with the *Sunday Times* (June 1962), Anthony Eden's attitude when he met Nasser briefly in Cairo was 'that he was talking to a junior official who could not be expected to understand international politics'. The governments of some African and Asian states still allowed themselves to be treated in this way, so the U.S.A. and Britain saw no reason to revise their attitude towards Egypt.

Nasser's neutralism gained a wholly new dimension with the Bandoeng Conference in April 1955. Meeting on equal terms with Pandit Nehru, Chou En-lai and other senior Asian statesmen, he could feel that his earlier forecasts about Egypt's potential role in the world were coming true. At the same time he was more convinced than ever that to play this role Egypt's hands ought not to be tied by any pact with the West. The wise and philosophical Nehru, the apostle of non-alignment, was a powerful influence on the young Egyptian officer and did much to widen and deepen his political vision. President Tito of Yugoslavia, who on the other side had defied the whole Communist bloc and got away with it, was the other living statesman able to strengthen and encourage Nasser's instinctive beliefs. Eventually, Nehru, Tito and Nasser came to be regarded as the three-cornered foundation of non-alignment.

After Bandoeng, Nasser took several defiant initiatives which further alarmed and angered the Western powers. In July 1955 he arranged a large-scale purchase of heavy Soviet arms through Czechoslovakia; in May 1956 he recognized Communist China. But the United States and Britain still hoped that he could be brought to heel; they held a strong card in the seventy million dollars they had agreed to lend Egypt to build the Aswan High Dam. The World Bank had offered a further 200 million, but this was conditional on the Anglo-American loan. There were strong pressures against helping Egypt to this extent in both Britain and the United States (from pro-Zionists, elements, old-fashioned imperialists, isolationists, etc.) so the brusque and insulting withdrawal of the offer was not politically difficult. The extent to which Eden influenced Dulles in the decision is still uncertain, but there is little doubt that both of them were confident Nasser would either fall from power as a result or at least become more pliable.

By July 1956, when the Suez crisis began, Nasser was well on his way to becoming the West's chief bogey-man. The Americans saw him as responsible for having let the Russians into the Middle East, while the British considered him a dangerous threat to their Middle East interests. The British Foreign Minister Mr Selwyn Lloyd was convinced, for instance, that Nasser had arranged the sacking of General Glubb, Chief of Staff of Jordan's Arab Legion, in February 1956. The French believed that Cairo's support was largely responsible for keeping the Algerian rebellion alive. All three governments disliked and distrusted Nasser personally, and their feelings reflected public opinion. Although the British Labour Party and the American Government officially opposed the Anglo-French invasion of Egypt and can both claim some credit for stopping it, there were only a few individuals in the West who were prepared to show active and positive sympathy for the country that had been invaded. Michael Foot and Mervin Jones in their *Guilty Men*, 1957 and Paul Johnson in his *The Suez War* were typical of left-wing British journalists in showing that they disliked Nasser's Egypt as much as they disliked the Tories.

After Suez, the American Government quickly threw away the credit that it had earned with Egypt by its hostility to the Suez adventure; it supported the Anglo-French economic blockade and then vigorously pursued the Cold War in the Middle East, which in effect meant backing all Nasser's opponents against him. The blockade forced Egypt to find markets for its cotton and economic aid for its industrialization programme in the Communist bloc, and this strengthened the argument that Nasser was 'going red' and taking Egypt with him.

Since 1957, Nasser's relations with the Western powers have improved in patches. Towards the end of the second Eisenhower administration, the State Department came to the conclusion not only that Nasser was not a Communist, but that he promised, in fact, the best defence against Communism in the Middle East. This revised policy was carried further after the election of President Kennedy, who came close to establishing cordial and confident relations with Nasser, and who was warmly admired by him in return. Between 1958 and 1964 the U.S.A. provided Egypt with over $1,000,000,000 of aid – mostly in cheap long-term loans under the PL 480 arrangement for the sale of surplus American foodstuffs. Kennedy's death came as a deep shock to Nasser and to all the Arabs who felt that they had lost the first American statesman with some sympathy for their point of view. They were not reassured when President Johnson, an American politician with less interest in foreign affairs than Kennedy, gave evidence of being much more sensitive to the importance of the American Jewish vote, and they felt their suspicions confirmed when the U.S. Ambassador to Egypt, John Badeau, whom Nasser liked and trusted, retired from diplomacy to Columbia University in the summer of 1964. Matters steadily deteriorated as Egypt gave increasing support to the Congolese rebels against Mr Tshombe's government, and in November the U.S.-assisted Belgian paratroop landing at Stanleyville was followed by the burning down of the Kennedy Memorial Library at the U.S. Embassy in Cairo by Congolese students reinforced by Egyptians. In December there was an incident between the Egyptian Minister of Supply and the new U.S. Ambassador in Cairo which seems to have been based on a misunderstanding but which convinced Nasser that the U.S. was trying to use their PL 480 food supplies to bring pressure on him to change his policies. His reaction was wholly characteristic. In his Port Said speech of 23 December he defiantly admitted that Egypt was sending arms to the Congolese rebels, proclaimed that it would continue to do so, and went on to tell the U.S. Ambassador to take a running jump at himself (the Arabic equivalent was to suggest that he should go and drink the Mediterranean and, if this was not enough, the Red Sea also).

All the powerful anti-Nasser forces in the U.S. rallied, and the House of Representatives passed a resolution to stop all further aid to Egypt. But the reaction of the State Department was even more significant. Both President Johnson and Secretary of State Dean Rusk were horrified that the U.S. Government's hands should be so tied in the Middle East. Stopping aid to Egypt would not only make America's Middle Eastern policy more inflexible, but was bound to fail in its object of persuading Nasser to change his policy. They managed to have the vote reversed in the Senate.

The realities of U.S.–Egyptian relations had reasserted themselves just in time. As John Badeau remarked in a wise and penetrating article for *Foreign Affairs* in January 1965:

Both Egypt and the United States need each other; their realistic national interests demand reasonably cooperative relations. That is why, despite the strains and vagaries of policy during the past decade, there has never been an irrevocable rupture.... So long as the United States has vital interests in Arab lands and the United Arab Republic has a role of influence and leadership, the two countries cannot escape doing business with each other. The question is whether they can be sufficiently mature, clear-sighted and patient to work out a gradually consistent and mutually profitable relationship.

From 1963 onwards, France ceased to be the Arab's *bête noire* among the Western powers. Arab support for the Algerians and France's diplomatic and military support for Israel (which were themselves related) made *rapprochement* impossible as long as the Algerian war continued, and Franco-Egyptian relations reached their lowest point with the trial for espionage of the French diplomats in the French Economic Mission to Egypt in the summer of 1962. But the Algerian settlement opened the way to a complete reorientation of French policy towards the Arabs. A French Ambassador returned to Cairo after five years, and France's ancient cultural affinity with Egypt began to reassert itself in numerous ways. Compared with the indecisive politicians of the Fourth Republic, President de Gaulle is a man that Nasser can understand and appreciate. He may not see eye to eye with him in all matters – such as France's right to carry out atomic tests in the Sahara – but these differences are more than outweighed by the other aspects of de Gaulle's foreign policy and in particular by his defiance of '*les Anglo-Saxons*'. The French President has already shown signs of being prepared to support Nasser in his demand for the removal of all the remaining British and American bases in the Middle East.

It is only with the British Government that there is very little sign of improvement, and this situation is unlikely to change as long as Britain keeps military bases in Aden, Bahrain and elsewhere on the fringes of Arabia. A Labour government has a slightly better chance of coming to an understanding with Nasser on these matters, but the Wilson administration seems as little inclined as its predecessor to accept that Egypt has any direct interest in them and should be party to any negotiations. At present there is almost complete antipathy between the two countries at the official level. On the one hand, Nasser is convinced, with some justification, that the British Government will support his enemies anywhere in the Arab world whether they are Yemeni royalists, feudal sheikhs or Baath socialists. On the other hand, the British Government, with equal justification, feels that Nasser will not rest until the last traces of British influence have been removed from the Middle East.

Yet in many ways the two countries are still close together. Even immediately after Suez, Englishmen rarely felt any personal hostility from Egyptians. On the cultural and professional level relations have remained reasonably good, and in 1965 there was a record number of over one thousand Egyptian students in Britain. The fact is that the British left an impression on Egypt which has not been wholly eradicated and probably never will be. Individual Egyptians, while denouncing British policy, often show admiration for, or at least a deep interest in, British institutions. Nasser himself is an example. In his speech at Port Said on 23 December 1962, the Sixth Anniversary of Victory Day, he said: '. . . in the past, when *The Times* said one word, the Prime Minister of the Kingdom of Egypt fell. Today they can do nothing but insult us.' Yet by his anger and his frequent references to recent articles in the *Daily Telegraph* and *The Times*, he shows clearly that he follows the British Press assiduously and is affected by what it says. Egypt no longer responds to British opinion, but it still reacts.

Egypt's relations with other Western European powers is

strikingly different. West Germany and Italy, for instance, are both playing an economic and technical role in Egypt of the greatest importance. In particular, German scientists and engineers are the basis of Egypt's rocket and jet fighter building programme. Many Egyptians, like most Arabs, admire the qualities of industriousness and efficiency which are regarded as characteristic of the German nation, and thousands of Egyptians have studied in Germany since the war – mostly engineering and science. Yet German–Egyptian relations never display anything like the intense feeling of Anglo-Egyptian relations. It is partly a cultural matter, for very few Egyptians have any knowledge of German literature, thought or institutions. But more than this, it is due to the close interweaving of British and Egyptian history for the past hundred years.

The nature of Egypt's relations with the Soviet Union is almost the exact converse of those with Britain. There is much greater harmony, but also far less passion. Since 1954, when Egypt began to turn towards neutralism (which in Egypt's case meant that it veered away from the West), Soviet foreign policy has generally been in agreement with Egypt's. The Czech arms deal in 1955 was vital to Egypt's pursuit of an independent foreign policy in defiance of the West because it broke the Western monopoly in arms supplies to the Middle East. After the Suez crisis it was Soviet technical and economic aid and Eastern bloc purchases of Egyptian cotton which not only saved Egypt from economic catastrophe but enabled it to continue its ambitious industrialization programme despite an almost total Western boycott. And all this is apart from the Soviet aid to Egypt for building the High Dam. When Mr Khrushchev visited Egypt in May 1964 it was announced that the Soviet Union would maintain and extend its aid with an additional £E. 100 million loan and assistance in reclaiming 200,000 *feddans* of desert land.

Egyptian engineers and industrial managers have sometimes found Soviet machinery and equipment less efficient than their Western equivalents; for this reason the Egyptian Government and the Egyptian contractor bought some Swedish drills and British 35-ton trucks for use at the High Dam. Furthermore, Soviet dumping of Egyptian cotton at a thirty per cent discount in Western European markets did some harm to the Egyptian economy in the late fifties and early sixties. But these two drawbacks do not alter the fact that the Soviet Union has made and is making a very large contribution to the Egyptian economy. If Egypt ever reaches its economic 'take-off' point, it will be largely due to the Soviet Union, and there is no reason to doubt President Nasser's sincerity when he declared, at the ceremony to mark the opening of the High Dam diversion canal, that the Egyptian people would never under any circumstances forget the help of Mr Khrushchev and the Soviet people.

Egypt's non-alignment policy, like that of other countries which have tried to follow the same course, has brought it into conflict with the Western bloc far more often than with the Eastern bloc. Over combating Western colonialism in its various forms and over getting rid of foreign bases in Africa and the Middle East, which have been President Nasser's chief concerns in foreign policy over the past ten years, he has been in entire accord with Mr Khrushchev. Soviet imperialism scarcely affects him. Its most flagrant example, the suppression of the Hungarian revolution, coincided with Suez, so that Nasser had little chance to consider it. Certainly where the U.S.S.R. and the Western powers confront each other outside Egypt's immediate sphere of interest, as in Cuba or Berlin, Nasser has taken care to emphasize his neutrality. In the Cuban crisis of September 1963, Egypt's concern was the same as that of everyone else: that it might lead to the Third World War.

There remains one potential source of conflict between the Egyptian and Soviet Governments – the activities of Communists in Egypt, in the Arab States and, to a lesser extent, among Egypt's non-Arab neighbours in Africa. It was this which brought the U.S.S.R. and Egypt close to a serious breach in 1959. After the crushing of an anti-Communist Arab nationalist uprising in Mosul, General Kassem leaned heavily on the Iraqi Communists for support, and Arab Communists elsewhere took heart, especially in neighbouring Syria where their organization had been suppressed and they had been forced underground since the union with Egypt. Nasser reacted vigorously. Speaking in Damascus on 11 March he said:

The Communists who have stirred up demonstrations to defame the leaders and people of the U.A.R. will find no one in the whole Arab world who will listen to them except their agents, for the Communists themselves are agents who neither believe in the liberty of their land or their nation but only do the bidding of outsiders.

Again and again while he was in Syria, Nasser returned to this theme. He accused the Iraqi leaders of having 'opened the gates of Baghdad to the Communists so that they might work against your Republic, assuming that they would be able to establish a Communist Fertile Crescent in which Baghdad would be a spring-board for Communism'.

For some time the Press and radio of Eastern European States had been criticizing the U.A.R. and Arab nationalism. Mr Khrushchev himself entered the field on 16 March 1959 when, at the signing of the Soviet–Iraqi technical and financial aid agreement, he remarked that 'the Iraqi Revolution of 14 July has gained the support of all progressive powers in the world'. He added that the anti-Communist policy adopted by President Nasser would not bring him victory and that 'when the U.A.R. President talks about Communism and Communists, he arms himself with the language of the imperialists'. He did go on to say, however, that relations between the U.S.S.R. and the U.A.R. would 'continue as heretofore'. This was clearly an assurance that Soviet aid to the U.A.R. was not going to be cut off.

President Nasser's reply was sharp: on 17 March he said: 'Mr Khrushchev's defence of Communists in our country is unacceptable to the Arab people. We do not interfere in the internal affairs of the Soviet Union and we do not support any section of the people there against another.'

The breach never went deeper than this largely because the Iraqi Communists failed. Until his downfall in February 1962, Kassem succeeded in maintaining a difficult balancing act with the two main political forces in Iraq, the Communists and Arab nationalists (which in this case were mainly Baathist). Whenever either group appeared to be becoming too powerful he slapped them down. The February 1963 revolt which was Baathist-led and decisively anti-Communist was followed by the widespread suppression of Communism in Iraq.

What would have happened if the Communists had succeeded in establishing the first Arab Communist State in Iraq must remain a matter of speculation. It is difficult to see how Nasser could have avoided adopting anti-Soviet policies, because a Communist Iraq, backed by the Soviet Union, would have struck at the root of his Arab nationalist ideals. As it happened, the issue did not arise, and there is no doubt that Nasser was deeply relieved, for it would have meant the virtual abandonment of non-alignment; but it is also unlikely that Mr Khrushchev shed many tears for the Iraqi Communists, who had shown themselves to be incompetent revolutionaries and had only succeeded in making themselves detested by all non-Communists in Iraq. An unstable and isolated Communist Iraq would have been poor compensation for the loss of Nasser's friendship and the enmity of all the other Arab states.

During 1959 and 1960 many hundreds of Egyptian Communists and 'progressives' were detained and imprisoned without trial, though many of these were middle-class intellectuals whose highly theoretical Marxism had never shown much sign of being translated into revolutionary action. Unlike the Syrian Communists, they hardly constituted a threat to the U.A.R., but they were paying the price for Communist activities elsewhere in the Arab world. In a speech on Education Day, 18 December 1961, President Nasser said:

We do not accept the return of capitalism or feudalism because they represent the rule of a minority, of one class; we have also declared that we do not accept the dictatorship of the proletariat expressed by Communism because this also means the domination of a small group.

This explains why he disagrees with Communist theory but not why he distrusts Communists. This, as he has said many times, is because they owe their allegiance to a movement which has its centre outside Egypt or the Arab world. When Arab Communism no longer seemed to threaten Arab nationalism, particularly after the February 1963 anti-Kassem revolution in Baghdad, Egyptian Communists and fellow-travellers were gradually released from the prison camps until by May 1964, when Mr Khrushchev visited Egypt, there was none left in detention.

It has been suggested that the Soviet Premier made this a condition of his visit, but this is unlikely, because the process of
releasing Communist detainees began at least a year before his
visit was arranged. Indeed, there is no evidence that the Soviet
Government ever tried to use the powerful means of pressure at
its disposal to secure the release of Egyptian Communists. On
the contrary it has implicitly advertised the fact that it has not,
in order to demonstrate that its aid to Egypt is 'without strings'.
On the other hand, President Nasser may well have decided on
the release of all Egyptian Communists before May 1964 as a
gesture of good will to his Soviet guest.

Mr Khrushchev's sixteen-day visit to Egypt in May 1964
showed at once how much he had in common with President
Nasser and how great was the gulf that divided them. On colonialism, neo-colonialism and the danger of foreign bases in the
Middle East they were agreed. When the Soviet Premier referred
to Israel as an imperialist base and expressed his support for the
Arab cause in Palestine and over the Jordan waters, his Egyptian
hosts were delighted. They were equally pleased when he praised
the socialist achievement of the Egyptian revolution. But when
he implied that Arab nationalism was only a stage on the road to
the Communist goal, they were more doubtful. Then President
Aref of Iraq, who was in Egypt for the ceremonies to mark the
end of work on the first stage of the High Dam, made a speech
from the same rostrum as the Soviet Premier in which he devoted
himself entirely to the theme of Arab nationalism, pointedly
avoiding any reference to the class war or other Marxist termino-
logy. Mr Khrushchev, obviously very irritated, responded with
a speech in which he declared that the only true union is based
on the workers and not on nationalism. He seemed to be imply-
ing that Arab nationalism was irrelevant and out of date.

President Nasser could not let this pass. In his private talks
with Mr Khrushchev he explained at length his concept of Arab
nationalism. In a speech he declared that the Arab nation had
been united only to be artificially divided and that the Arabs still
had one conscience and one mind.

The Soviet and Egyptian leaders had publicly disagreed on a
fundamental point. But there is reason to believe that President

Nasser was not altogether displeased that this had happened, for it served once again to emphasize his non-alignment. It is quite possible that he invited President Aref to Aswan in order to exhibit for Mr Khrushchev's benefit an uncompromisingly Muslim Arab nationalist viewpoint.

The fall of Mr Khrushchev was as much of a shock to Nasser and his associates as the death of President Kennedy. It was under Khrushchev's leadership that the Soviet Union had become a Middle Eastern power, and it was Khrushchev who had taken and maintained the decision to place so many Soviet eggs in the Egyptian basket. His personal relationship with Nasser was as close as with any other non-Communist leader. Soon after his fall, ominous reports leaked from Moscow of resentment that he had involved the U.S.S.R. so heavily in Egypt on his own initiative and in particular that he had made Nasser a Hero of the Soviet Union without consulting his colleagues in the Kremlin.

Nasser hastily despatched Field-Marshal Amer to Moscow to see the new Soviet leaders, and he returned with assurances that Soviet aid would continue as before. This was confirmed by the Soviet Deputy Premier Alexander Shelepin when he visited Egypt in December.

There was never a serious possibility that the Soviet Union would do otherwise. If it were to cut back its aid to Egypt and force it to revise its Second Five-Year Plan drastically, the damage to its own reputation among the under-developed countries would be incalculable. On the other hand, it was never a very realistic supposition that Egypt might go further and ask the Communist bloc to replace all Western aid, including American surplus foodstuffs; still less, that the Soviets would agree. The Egyptians could hardly expect the U.S.S.R. to add anything to the recently given £E. 100 million of long-term credits, and they know that it cannot and will not provide hard currency in cash. The most they can hope for is a relaxation in the repayment terms of Egypt's rouble debts.

It is often said in the West that Egypt is generally so much more sympathetic to Soviet than to Western views that it cannot properly be called non-aligned. But no one who has had any contact with Nasser can be unaware of his overriding desire to keep

Egypt's freedom of action uninfluenced by any outside power. Suggestions that he is a crypto-Communist carrying out the Kremlin's orders have always been tendentious nonsense, and it is hard to see how he could go further to prove it than by his actions in 1959. If Egypt's Marxist political prisoners have been released and in some cases restored to influential positions in the Press and universities, it is because he believes that they have something valuable to contribute to the Egyptian State and that they are no longer dangerous. It is possible that Mr Khrushchev suggested that it would be a good idea to release the Communists, but if Nasser had felt that he was in any way being threatened, his instinctive reaction would have been to refuse.

With the constant change and development of international relations, non-alignment cannot mean the adopting of a position which is exactly equidistant from two world power blocs. The forty-six nations calling themselves non-aligned that met at Cairo in October 1964 exhibited a wide range of views on international questions. In many cases Egypt took a position that was moderate from the West's point of view. But there are several good reasons why Nasser's Egypt is likely to remain on better terms with the East than the West for some years to come.

First – Egypt's unremitting opposition to colonial remnants and military bases in the Arab world. This at present only affects Britain and the United States, and there is a good chance that this cause of friction will be removed before very long as both the protectorates and bases are liquidated.

Second – Egypt's support for radical revolutionary movements against conservative pro-Western regimes in the Middle East and Africa. This is not such a serious matter today when so many African and Arab States have governments that profess to be non-aligned and socialist. But the Congo shows how this can still be a source of bitter disagreement with the West.

Third – Egypt's socialist policies, which have liquidated almost all the formerly immense Western economic interests in Egypt. The fact that in many cases compensation has not yet been paid is one of the chief causes of hostility to Egypt in the West.

Fourth – Israel. It is not so much that the creation of Israel is still held against the West (the Soviet Union bears almost as much responsibility) as that the Western powers have adopted a policy of guaranteeing Israel's survival and strengthening its defences. Although something has been done to right the balance in recent years, Israel still receives far more aid and arms *per capita* than do the Arab States. This is the consequence of the attempt by the West to maintain a balance of power between two million Israelis and fifty million Arabs. The case of the secret West German arms deal with Israel is only one example of the trouble this will cause. Ironically, it is now France that seems the most successful of all Western powers in maintaining its relations with both Israelis and Arabs.

On these four points the Soviet Union has no reason to quarrel with Egypt. It is unlikely that it wishes to see Israel liquidated, and there is evidence that Mr Khrushchev told the Egyptians so in May 1964. But the U.S.S.R. is not going to do anything positive to help Israel economically or militarily.

6 The African Circle

As for the Second Circle – the African Continent circle – I should say without the necessity of going into details, that we cannot under any circumstances, even if we wanted to, stand aloof from the terrible and terrifying battle now raging in the heart of that continent between five million whites and two hundred million Africans. We cannot stand aloof for one important and obvious reason – we ourselves are in Africa.

Surely the people of Africa will continue to look to us – we who are the guardians of the continent's north-eastern gate and constitute the link between Africa and the outside world.

We certainly cannot, under any circumstances, relinquish our responsibility to help to our utmost in spreading the light of knowledge and civilization as far as the very depths of the virgin jungles of the continent.   *Philosophy of the Revolution*, 1954

While our people believe in Arab unity, they also believe in a pan-African movement and an Afro-Asian solidarity.

National Charter, 1962

Egyptians tend to show impatience when they are asked whether they feel more African or Arab. 'Nobody asks the Algerians or the Tunisians,' they say. 'Why do they pick on us?' No one, it is true, questions whether France is Mediterranean or North European; the obvious answer is that it is both. Nevertheless, there are very good reasons why doubts have been raised over whether pan-Arabism and pan-Africanism are fully compatible in Egypt's case.

As we have already seen, twenty years ago most people, including the majority of Egyptians, did not regard Egypt as an Arab State at all. Until the Revolution, the unity of Egypt and the Sudan under the Egyptian crown was still the chief aim of Egyptian foreign policy. But if Egypt was primarily African at that time, its interest was localized in the north-east of the continent. The young Colonel Nasser in his book on the Egyptian Revolution had a vision of what would happen in the vast colonialized mass of the African States, but even he did not foresee that within ten years the Heads of State or their representatives from thirty-three independent countries in the Organization of African Unity would be meeting in Cairo. In 1954 pan-Africanism was still the palest dream. One of the first acts of the Egyptian revolutionary officers was to drop their country's claim to the Sudan in order to make way for Sudanese independence, and if they were disappointed that the new Sudanese Government never opted for union with Egypt they did not brood over the matter. The evacuation of the last British troops from the Canal Zone in 1954 left Egypt's hands free to pursue an independent policy, and its energies were directed in the main towards the Asian Arab States and the Arab nationalist movement.

The history of Sudanese–Egyptian relations is a subject for major study in itself, but curiously they have never been an important concern of Nasser's Egypt. After Ismail el-Azhari's government had turned its back on the political unity of the Nile Valley, Egypt continued to try and influence Sudanese politics, but its heart was no longer in it. In February 1958 it moved troops into two slices of territory on the Sudanese borders to which it lays claim, and one result was the victory of the anti-Egyptian Umma Party in the subsequent general elections. During the six years of military rule in the Sudan, from 1958 to 1964, Egypt's relations with the country were formally correct but far from cordial. Egypt felt that the Sudan was under excessive Western (especially British) influence, and its main concern was to reach an agreement on the Nile Waters – achieved in November 1959 – in order to start building the High Dam.

In the euphoric period which followed the successful civilian *coup* against the military in October 1964, the Sudanese caretaker Premier, Serr el-Khatem Khalifa, paid a goodwill visit to Cairo, and a new Sudanese–Egyptian trade agreement was signed. But the Egyptians still did not rate very high their chances of influencing any Sudanese elections in their favour, especially as the Umma Party seemed once again in the ascendant and there was no obvious pro-Egyptian opposition to support.

Below the official level the two countries still have close contacts. There are more students from the Sudan than from any other Arab State at Egyptian schools and universities, and most Egyptians, if pressed, will still say that the only natural union for their country is with the Sudan. But in practical terms, this seems a very remote possibility. Partly for historical reasons, the Sudanese fear that the Egyptians wish to dominate them and they resent the slightly patronizing 'elder sister' attitude that individual Egyptians tend to show towards them. Any Sudanese political party which campaigned on a 'union with Egypt' platform would not get very far.

Egypt did not forget Africa in its new emphasis on the Arab world. As Nasser had written, it could not 'stand aloof from the terrible and terrifying battle'. Cairo, which was already a home for refugee nationalist leaders from North Africa, now gave hospitality to others from south of the Sahara. Felix Moumié of the Cameroons and John Kale of the Uganda National Congress were among the many who established bureaux in Cairo. In practice the head of any nationalist party or group involved in the struggle against colonial rule is given facilities to open an office in Cairo, a salary of £E. 100 a month and free tickets to travel wherever he likes. In some cases where the nationalist movement is divided, as are the South Africans between the African National Congress and the Pan-Africanist Congress, both groups have bureaux in Cairo. The U.A.R. at first regarded the left-wing U.P.L.A. as representing the Angolan nationalist movement, but later switched to official recognition of Holden Roberto's Provisional Government together with the majority of States in the O.A.U. In general, however, Egyptian policy has been to welcome the representatives of all nationalist movements, and where any African party or group has no representative in Cairo it is through its own choice and not the Egyptian Government's.

Since many of these movements have now been successful in winning independence for their countries, the activities of their Cairo bureaux have declined; but over the past ten years the

African Association, founded in 1955 to group them together, has played an important role in the cause of African freedom. Above all, Cairo was ideally suited to provide facilities for African nationalist propaganda. Many of the bureaux published their own pamphlets and periodicals – they now jointly publish a well-produced magazine, *al-Rabitat-al-Afriqiya* – and they were also given regular time for broadcasting on Cairo radio. At present the 'Voice of Africa from Cairo Calling East, Central and South Africa' broadcasts for four hours daily in Amharic, Swahili, Lingala, Sesotho, Nyanja, Somali and English. The 'Voice of Africa from Cairo Calling West Africa' broadcasts for four hours in French, Fulani, English, and Hausa.

Many of these broadcasts have been violent, inflammatory and unscrupulous. The Swahili programmes encouraging the 'Mau-Mau' movement at the height of the Kenya emergency aroused special resentment in Britain, but the Egyptians could well feel that they were justified in permitting them when Jomo Kenyatta, the man who was accused of leading the movement, convicted and imprisoned, emerged as the first Prime Minister of independent Kenya.

During the past ten years, also, Egypt has played an increasingly important role as an educational centre for young Africans, comparable indeed to Britain, France, the United States and the Soviet Union. In 1964 there were about 2,000 government-sponsored non-Arab African students in Egypt. Of these, 400 were receiving Egyptian Government scholarships at secular universities, and 250 at al-Azhar. In addition, there were several hundred more who had come on their own initiative.

In the non-independent states the authorities have usually frowned on the students coming to Cairo, which they regarded, with justice, as a forcing house of anti-colonialist ideas. Often these students had to find their own ways of getting to Egypt. Most of them had to live and work in crowded and difficult conditions. But Egypt provided them with an opportunity they would not otherwise have had.

Egyptian teachers are working throughout the continent, though the great majority of them are concentrated in the Arab states. In 1964 there were 751 in Algeria (shortly to rise to 2,000),

825 in Libya, 740 in Sudan. But there were also 373 in Somalia (including 144 Arabic teachers from al-Azhar), eight in Mali, eight in Sierra Leone, three in Kenya. In most of the independent African States Egypt maintains a cultural centre. It is doing its best to encourage the knowledge of Arabic throughout the continent, and naturally it finds this task easiest among the Muslim populations.

As a radiating centre of radical anti-imperialist ideas and as a revolutionary example, Egypt played a key role in the African continent's struggle for independence between 1954 and 1964. But never at any time during this period was it politically involved in Africa to anything like the extent that it was in the Arab world. This was true even when Egyptian troops were present in the Congo for a short time as part of the U.N. force and during the short life of the Casablanca group (Egypt, Morocco, Mali, Guinea, Ghana) between 1961 and 1963, when it looked as if this minority of radical independent African States might act as a pace-setter for the rest of the continent. The Casablanca group went as far as to establish on paper a joint military command and a common market, but it never had any organic life of its own and soon fell apart through its internal contradictions. By the time of the Addis Ababa conference in May 1963, when the O.A.U. was established, President Nasser had already renounced any idea that Egypt should take the lead in the movement towards African unity.

At the Cairo conference of the O.A.U. in July 1964, he was a moderating, one might almost say a conservative, influence. He made it clear that Egypt would make no attempt to outbid President Nkrumah's proposals for immediate continental unity. Probably keeping his own unfortunate experience with Arab federations in mind, he warned against creating the constitutional form of African unity before achieving the 'Spirit of African Unity'. As he said, 'With the articles of constitutions we might find ourselves before a façade lacking the third dimension'. The policy which had divided Africa between the radicals (Casablanca) and moderates (Monrovia) had been decisively abandoned. During 1963 and 1964 Egypt painstakingly tried to make friends with the generally rather conservative governments of the former French colonies. Until 1963 it did not even have diplomatic relations with any of them, but by 1964 it had established them with Senegal, Congo (Brazzaville), Dahomey, and Niger. It was an uphill task, and many of these States remained suspicious. Several Heads of State from francophobe countries such as the Ivory Coast, Upper Volta and the Central African Republic, failed to come to the Cairo conference, and their delegations played a subdued role compared with the Addis Ababa meeting of the year before. President Nasser himself cannot conceal the fact that he feels closer to the 'radical' African leaders such as Sekou Touré and Nkrumah (even though he disagrees with the latter on several major points) than to more conservative monarchs and presidents. But he is not willing to take sides openly in Africa in the way that he is still quite prepared to do in the Arab world.

When Syria seceded from the union with Egypt in September 1961, many people thought that Egypt might turn its back on the Arab world in dudgeon. Scores of articles appeared arguing that since Egypt is the creation of the Nile, which rises in the heart of the African continent, its natural interests lie southward rather than to the north and east. But Egypt did not turn its back, and it was never very likely that it would. Language, which is more important to the Arabs than to any other race, is one of the reasons. When he talks, Nasser can reach the heart of the Arabs in a way that he cannot hope to do with the Africans south of the Sahara, and this is no doubt why, when he spoke at the Cairo O.A.U. conference, his appeal was mainly directed to his audience's heads.

Israel is another factor keeping Egypt tied to the Arab world. However much Nasser might wish that they were not, the Palestine problem and the possibility of war with Israel are overriding considerations in all Egypt's policies. For other African countries, including even the Arab States of the Maghreb, this is not so. On the contrary, many of them have established diplomatic relations and friendly links with Israel. Israelis run cooperatives in Tanganyika and build hotels in Kenya. Israeli agricultural technicians and advisers are working in many of the newly independent African states. Israel offers hundreds of scholarships to Africans for study in Israeli schools and universities. African politicians visit Israel in a steady stream.

There is not much that Egypt can do in retaliation. The Arab League has talked about combating Israeli penetration in Africa, but in reality the Arabs can only hope to offer what the Israelis are offering in larger quantities. The argument that all the Arab leaders who spoke at the Cairo conference put forward in one form or another – that the Israelis are comparable to the white South Africans or Southern Rhodesian settlers, only worse, because they turned a million indigenous people out of their homes to take their land – aroused little response among the sub-Saharan Africans, although it may make some impression in time. In general Palestine seems remote from Central Africa, and unless the Israelis over-reach themselves by becoming too influential in any one country (as they seemed about to do at one time in Ghana) the Africans will not regard them as a neo-colonialist menace so much as a source of valuable assistance. At Cairo, President Nasser wisely announced at the beginning of the conference that the Arabs would not put forward any anti-Israeli resolution, and only Sekou Touré and Nkrumah expressed sympathy with the Arab case on Palestine. The Prime Minister of Malawi, Dr Hastings Banda, was more typical; when he referred to Suez, he spoke of Egypt's having faced 'the British, French and others'. Malawi receives substantial technical help from the Israelis, and presumably Banda did not wish to offend them by mentioning them as aggressors; although why the British should not have been exempt for the same reason is not clear.

Before leaving Cairo after the O.A.U. conference in July 1964, President Nyerere said that the conference had been 'proof of the unity of the African continent and refuted the false propaganda which divided it into black Africa and Arab Africa'. Undoubtedly, some quarters have been interested in encouraging non-Arab Africans to feel that the Arabs have not lost their slave-trading mentality. But it cannot be denied that many black Africans would have this feeling even without encouragement from outsiders. North Africans are much lighter skinned than the sub-Saharans; on the Mediterranean littoral many are as fair as Europeans. They are also generally more advanced economically, so that in a sense the African continent reflects the north–south division of the world between developed and under-developed countries. This alone would be enough to create suspicion of the Arabs among the other Africans.

The problem must, however, be kept in perspective. There is no racial feeling between Arabs and non-Arabs in Africa which can be compared with that between Anglo-Saxon Protestant races and non-whites. The fact that Islam is a colour-blind religion has something to do with it and also, incidentally, accounts for Muslim missionary successes in Africa. The absence among the Arabs of sexual puritanism, which is the basis of much Anglo-Saxon racial prejudice, is another factor. Nevertheless, it would be wrong to say that Africans from south of the Sahara are never in the north made conscious of their racial difference. As one South African political refugee living in Cairo remarked: 'I have not encountered racial discrimination in Egypt. But there is plenty of racial awareness.'

Some of the Asian Arabs, it is only fair to report, have a racial awareness that denigrates the Egyptians. The Parti Populaire Syrienne, which flourished in the 1930s and 1940s, was strongly tinged with ideas of Syrian Arab racial superiority. After the formation of the Syrian–Egyptian union in 1958, one Syrian intellectual remarked: 'This is the first case in history of a black nation colonizing a white one.' His tongue was only half in his cheek.

If the Sahara is still in some measure a barrier, it is one that is steadily being lowered by contacts across it. Several African leaders who attended the O.A.U. conference expressed thanks to their hosts with a warmth which went far beyond the normal requirements of protocol, and it was clear that they had been favourably impressed – and perhaps surprised – by their reception in Egypt and what they had found there. In particular, Egypt was able to make use of the conference to establish much closer relations with the East Africans. After visiting the High Dam, President Nyerere of Tanganyika said: 'There are many and un-limited opportunities for joint effort and fruitful cooperation between the United Arab Republic and the sons of East Africa in carrying out numerous schemes to benefit from the Nile and its sources.'

What impressed the African leaders most about Egypt was the extent to which it had progressed towards achieving a state of self-sustained economic growth, ultimately the only basis of true political independence. This is not to say that Egypt is approaching economic self-sufficiency, which is something that very few countries can attain. But it is true that Egypt is today less at the mercy of politically directed outside economic pressures than any other independent African State. This is partly because it has been successful in keeping its sources of economic assistance spread widely over East and West. But it is also due to its own progress in industrialization since the Revolution and particularly during the past five years. A large and impressive Egyptian Industrial Exhibition was timed to coincide with the O.A.U. conference. Several African leaders were inclined to link this achievement with political stability and consequently with Egypt's lack of political parties. One of the first things that Jomo Kenyatta did on his return to Nairobi was to announce that he wanted Kenya to become a one-party State. All this tends to confirm that Egypt's role in Africa is likely to be one of example and inspiration. It is unlikely to involve political leadership, even of the indirect kind, which its natural preponderance in the Arab world allows it to undertake. Africans will come to Cairo for education. African nationalists from South Africa and the remaining colonial territories will continue to receive money and invaluable opportunities to conduct propaganda for their cause. Egypt's financial contribution to the Liberation Committee of Nine set up at Addis Ababa was substantially the largest. But it is in the possibility of becoming the Japan of Africa (the major industrial power of the 1960s, not the imperialist Japan of the 1930s) that Egypt's real opportunity lies.

Egypt has only just begun to penetrate Africa with manufactured goods. In the first half of 1964 total Egyptian exports to the continent amounted to just over £E. 3 million, compared with just under £E. 2 million in 1962. This is still only a little over one per cent of Egypt's total exports. A Ministry of Economy statement on African trade in July 1964 announced that Egypt could offer cotton textiles, ready-made clothing, pipes, tyres, shoes, canned foodstuffs, bicycles, leather goods, iron, reinforced rods, electric refrigerators, rice, onions and garlic.

Obviously, Egyptian-manufactured goods will have difficulty in competing with the products of the more advanced industrial nations unless they are substantially cheaper, which in general they are not. Egyptian cotton textiles, which are of good quality, are undercut by Indian, Japanese and Hong Kong textiles made from cheaper short staple cotton. One day Egypt may take the step of importing some of these cheap cotton strains to mix with its own, but so far it has refused to do so for fear of introducing new plant diseases.

At present, Egypt's best trading opportunities in Africa are with countries which are short of hard currencies, a situation likely to confront most of the newly independent States as they adopt ambitious development projects. Already Egypt has concluded trade and payments agreements with Algeria, Cameroons, Ethiopia, Ghana, Guinea, Kenya, Libya, Mali, Morocco, Niger, Somalia, the Sudan and Tunisia. It has made loans to Mali, Guinea, Somalia and Algeria, mostly in the form of capital goods. In Algeria it has undertaken to build an entire textile factory. But not all of these loans have yet been taken up, even when made several years ago. One obstacle to Egypt's developing bilateral trade with these countries is that very few of them have products which Egypt wants to import, although with the development of heavy industry in the second Five-Year Plan its demand for minerals and other raw materials is likely to increase.

Egypt's challenge and opportunity in Africa now lies in the economic sphere. It has a head-start in industrialization over all the other independent African States (except for the Republic of South Africa) and as a result of the High Dam it will soon have a substantial surplus of engineers and agriculturalists. This, incidentally, is the only effective way in which it can challenge Israel's influence in Africa. It has a long way to go, of course, before it will be considered seriously as a supplier of manufactured goods; but at a time when the African States are becoming increasingly concerned with neo-colonialism and their economic subordination to the advanced industrial States, Egypt has the immense advantage of having pioneered the anti-imperialist movement in Africa. Even Egypt, however, cannot take its anti-imperialist credentials for granted. It can influence and encourage the other African States, but any attempt to dominate them would be immediately resented and exploited by Egypt's enemies.

7 Human Resources

Wealthy Europeans who came to Egypt at the turn of the last century to enjoy the winter season occasionally observed that although Egypt's climate was healthy its people were not. In fact the inhabitants of the Nile Valley were among the most miserable and disease-ridden in the world. Since then, and especially since the Revolution, great advances have been made in raising the social standards of the mass of the Egyptian people. No moderately objective observer would deny either that there has been a great change for the better or that a vast amount remains to be done.

Socialized medicine or a comprehensive national health service for all citizens is the ultimate aim of the Egyptian Government. The National Charter states:

The right of each citizen to medical care, whether treatment or medicine, should not be a commodity for sale or purchase. It should be a guaranteed right independent of any price. Medical care should be within the reach of every citizen, in every part of the country and under easy conditions. Health insurance must be extended to cover all citizens.

Article 20 of the March 1964 constitution embodies the same idea. But no one should be under any illusion that this goal will be speedily reached. In view of the extremely low level of personal incomes, the great majority of the population will for many years be quite unable to make any national health insurance contribution. Almost the entire burden will have to be borne by the State, and because of the very low health standards of the rural population the cost will be enormous. However, a start has been made with government employees, and by the end of 1964, three million of them were included in a comprehensive insurance scheme. It should now be possible to include all employees and urban workers in a scheme financed by both employers and workers, and ultimately to extend this to the countryside. The problem is that in the meantime the disparity in social standards between town and rural area will be made wider.

The health of the *fellahin* is appallingly bad. Sixty per cent of them suffer from bilharziasis, the terrible debilitating disease caused by the water parasite bilharzia which penetrates the human skin in its larval form and eventually attacks the bladder, liver and kidneys. Ankylostoma, the earth parasite, is less common and more harmful than bilharzia, but since it lodges in the intestines rather than the body wall it is easier to treat. As a result of these two diseases, most of the *fellahin* spend years of their lives feeling weak and exhausted. The fact that they are undernourished also ensures that they almost never enjoy their full strength after adolescence.

Bilharzia remains the great scourge and the most difficult to eradicate, but there has been encouraging progress in controlling other diseases which used to be common in Egypt. Tuberculosis is much reduced, and there is good ground for hoping that malaria will be eliminated altogether in the near future. Less than ten years ago it seemed that all Egyptian children suffered from eye diseases, but through regular examination and penicillin ointments the incidence is now below ten per cent. Free midday meals for Egypt's 3.5 million schoolchildren are doing much to build up their health and resistance to disease.

Although a start had been made before the Revolution in establishing rural health centres, the programme has since been enormously expanded and speeded up. Since experience has shown that villagers will not go more than five kilometres for treatment, the aim is to establish 2,500 new rural health units within the next five years, each serving 5,000 people within a radius of three kilometres. By 1964 about 800 of these had been opened, in addition to 168 comprehensive treatment units for endemic diseases and 275 combined units which all include health sections.

In the drive to raise the health standards of the rural population the provision of free medical care and medicines is only part of the problem. The attitude of the people themselves towards disease and infection has to be changed. Ignorance is mainly responsible for the infant mortality rate, which has been reduced but remains very high. Officially it was 105 per 1,000 in 1962, but because many births and infant deaths are never recorded the rate is probably higher than this. In some of the villages it is at least 200 per 1,000.

One of the regime's most remarkable achievements has been the provision of clean drinking-water to almost all the villages. By 1966 the entire rural population of seventeen million will have access to clean water, compared with only two million at the time of the Revolution. But this is not enough, for many of the villagers still prefer to use the river water to which they have been so long accustomed. It will take time to persuade them that the life-giving Nile can be harmful.

In 1951–2 the Egyptian Public Health budget was £E. 10.1 million. In 1963–4 it was £E. 31.2 million, and in 1964–5 £E. 44.3 million. In 1951 there were 5,200 doctors, or one for every 4,000 inhabitants. In 1964 there were 13,000, or one for every 2,000 inhabitants. In 1962 there were over 57,000 beds in all the treatment establishments in the country, or one to every 482 inhabitants, compared with one to every 600 inhabitants in 1952. The 1964–5 budget provided for the establishment of three central hospitals, five general hospitals, two mental disease hospitals, six infant welfare centres, an infantile paralysis institution and three chest disease hospitals.

In its number of doctors and hospital beds, Egypt is now fairly well off compared with many countries at a similar stage of economic development. The medical profession enjoys high prestige, and many of the brightest students take up medicine. There are now two-and-a-half times as many doctors as there were in 1952, and inevitably this rapid increase has caused some decline in standards of training. But no very high level of skill is required to deal with the basic needs of the mass of the population; and the government's decision to make two years' service in the countryside compulsory for all qualified doctors after internship has been a major contribution towards tackling these needs. Extended health services combined with education, which is equally important, should produce a steady improvement in Egypt's health standards over the coming years.

The emphasis on sports and physical training in schools and summer youth camps has done much to improve the physique of the younger generation, and this is all the more necessary since the drift to the towns and the improved incomes and diet of the urban workers threaten to spread the well-known obesity of the Egyptian urban bourgeoisie – which has reached the proportions of a minor social evil – to the working class. At present the *fellahin* are debilitated by disease but have fine physiques.

The government has to face the prospect of an acceleration in the rate of population increase. In the 1930s this rate was between 1–1.5 per cent annually. Now it is over 2.5 per cent, but this is still lower than in some South American countries and if the infant mortality rate continues to fall, as it is most likely to do, Egypt must expect a net annual increase of three per cent, or one million new people a year, in the 1970s.

The problem created by Egypt's population increase is sometimes over-dramatized, with a million additional Egyptian mouths each year swallowing any extra food that can be grown in the New Valley or on land reclaimed from the desert. Obviously if this were so the thirty per cent increase in cropped area which the High Dam will achieve would soon be exhausted. But Egypt is not self-sustaining in food and would be foolish to try and become so except in time of war. Its economic future depends upon its being able to export agricultural products, such as cotton, vegetables, fruit and manufactured goods. During the past few years the gross national product has been increasing faster than the population, and there has been no fall in *per capita* income. Food imports have risen much faster than the population, which means that at least some of the people (mostly in the towns) are eating better than before. There is nothing wrong in this, provided that Egypt can pay for the imports, and this depends to a large extent on continued U.S. assistance in the form of surplus wheat under PL 480.

Nevertheless, Egypt does have a serious population problem, since it cannot provide sufficient employment for the rapidly growing labour force or raise the social standard of the mass of the population while the women are exhausted and prematurely aged through child-bearing. At present there is underemployment in both towns and countryside, but the problem is more intractable in the country. Although there is still no sign of a fall in the birth-rate of town-dwellers, except among the middle classes, it is most likely that middle-class attitudes will spread rapidly among the new industrial workers. In the villages, on the other hand, there seems to be no difference between the birth-rate of the more prosperous and of the poorer *fellahin*. Both are affected by the same considerations which are partly economic, since children can work in the cotton fields and provide a kind of insurance against old age, and partly traditional. They do not believe – as countless village proverbs illustrate – that man should interfere with God's decision as to how many children he shall have.

One interesting government survey undertaken about three years ago showed that inbreeding had a marked effect on the birth-rate. In villages where it was normal practice for first cousins to marry, the rate of conception was lower – while the rates of miscarriage and infant mortality were substantially higher – than in villages where it was not. This presents a problem. For social reasons inbreeding should obviously be discouraged, but the result would be a further acceleration in population growth.

It was not until ten years after the Revolution that President Nasser publicly advocated family planning. It seems that he took some time to make up his own mind on the matter. However pressing the arguments may be, it is always difficult for a leader with ambitious ideas of his nation's destiny to advocate restricting its manpower. In Egypt, as in China, there is a widespread suspicion that Western experts advocate birth-control for the developing nations so as to further their own imperialist purposes. Finally, although no senior Muslim leader in Egypt has ever challenged the government over birth-control, their underground opposition cannot be ignored.

The National Charter made itself quite clear:

This [population] increase constitutes the most dangerous obstacle that faces the Egyptian people in their drive towards raising the levels of income and production in an effective and efficient way ... family planning deserves the most sincere efforts supported by modern scientific methods ... regardless of the effects which may result from the experiment ...

This heralded an immediate change in the public attitude to the problem, which was discussed widely in the Press. Wisely the government decided that the first necessity was to find out more about what the mass of the people thought, and several surveys were conducted by university groups and the Ministry of Social Affairs.

Some experimental birth-control clinics were established. Near Alexandria out of 1,400 families who were asked to try oral contraceptive pills 400 agreed, and after seventeen months the experiment was reported to be sixty per cent successful. In May 1964 the Ministry of Social Affairs decided to establish birth-control clinics in all parts of the country, and by using social centres already in existence it was hoped to keep the cost down to £E. 700,000 and finance the scheme out of the Ministry's ordinary budget.

Many Egyptians feel that this does not go far enough. They say a Minister of Family Planning should be appointed and a nation-wide campaign promoted with the use of radio, television and cinema, as well as – if possible – the support of religious sheikhs in their Friday sermons. Only this, they say, would have any real prospect of changing mass attitudes. That a change is necessary was clear from one experimental clinic in the suburbs of Cairo. Of the twenty-two women who first visited the clinic, four wanted to stop having children while the rest wanted to have more because they were afraid that their husbands would divorce them. In February 1965 the National Assembly debated the subject at length, and the government announced a massive increase in the distribution of oral contraceptive pills.

Easy divorce is an important factor behind the high birth-rate. Polygamy bears little responsibility, since its incidence in Egypt is now below four per cent. But the divorce rate is over thirty per cent for the country as a whole and higher than this in the cities. There is no doubt that this increases child-bearing, for one of the most common causes of divorce is the desire of the male to have more children. The highest divorce rates are among very young married couples, and an investigation carried out by the Cairo weekly *al-Musawar* in June 1964 showed that seventy per cent of these early marriages in one industrial area of Cairo ended in failure. *Al-Musawar* launched a powerful campaign for the raising of the legal age of marriage from its present level of sixteen for girls and eighteen for boys to eighteen and twenty-one. There is little doubt that if such a law could be enforced it would do much to raise the social standards of the majority of the people. *Al-Musawar's* investigation showed that it was only when the parents married after the age of twenty-five that the children went to primary school. But enforcement would be difficult especially in the country where even the existing law is now widely evaded as parents register false dates of birth for the children they want to marry off.

The whole question of family planning and the effort to raise social and educational standards is intimately bound up with the status of women. This has been slowly but steadily improving in Egypt since the First World War, and there has been some acceleration since the Revolution. While there has been nothing comparable to the drastic laws to emancipate women of Kemalist Turkey, it is quite probable that Egypt's more gradualist approach will achieve more permanent results. The pace has never been so fast as to cause a counter-reaction.

Once again the National Charter has stated the principle:

Woman must be regarded as equal to man and she must therefore shed the remaining shackles that impede her free movement, so that she may play a constructive and profoundly important part in shaping the life of the country.

But as in other matters Nasser has recognized the strength of conservative feeling and has waited until the idea of women's equality had begun to be accepted by a much broader section of the population than a highly educated minority before stating it as a principle of the Revolution. Thus it was not until Mr and Mrs Khrushchev's visit to Egypt in May 1964 that photographs of Mrs Nasser accompanying her husband and the Soviet guests on numerous public occasions appeared in the

Cairo Press, although she had previously been photographed with the President on visits to Yugoslavia.

Conservative opinion was able to express itself during the debates of the National Congress of Popular Powers on the National Charter. The influential Cairo daily *al-Ahram*, and its sceptical cartoonist Salah Jahin, satirized these views and in particular one al-Azhar sheikh who had demanded that all women should be obliged to wear the veil. This led to a demonstration of Azhar students outside *al-Ahram*'s offices. *Al-Ahram* published an apology, but on the principle it was unrepentant, and in general the whole press has done much to promote the idea of female equality. Each year now it is possible to observe a higher proportion of women employed in schools, in factories and offices and in the growing tourist industry. There is a substantial number of women doctors, university teachers and lawyers, and in June 1964 a proposal to appoint some female judges aroused very little opposition. Egypt's first woman Minister, Dr Hikmat Abou Zeid, was appointed in 1962, and perhaps inevitably most of her energies came to be directed towards raising the status of women. The public had already become accustomed to having a few female members of parliament with the National Assemblies of 1956-8 and 1960-1, and in March 1964 eight out of the twenty-five women candidates in the general election were successful.

The strongest single factor behind the gradual emancipation of women in Egypt has been the growing acceptance of their right to equal educational opportunities with men. The proportion of girls in primary and secondary schools is now over thirty-seven per cent, compared with ten per cent in 1913. In 1961-2, twenty-six per cent of university students were girls. The biggest obstacle to their emancipation, on the other hand, is underemployment among the male population, which limits the employment of women even in the jobs where they are more productive and efficient than men. Ultimately it will be the social independence provided by wages which will do most to liberate the Egyptian woman.

Parallel with the increasing opportunities for women to show their independence, there has been a slow but marked relaxation in the severely conservative social customs governing the relations between the sexes. For many years now the veil has not been the symbol of segregation. It has never been common in the countryside and it is now rare in the cities (rarer than in Syria or among Lebanese Muslims). But until very recently Egyptian girls were kept in a kind of moral purdah, which perhaps was worse. Any unmarried girl who was seen talking alone to a man, even within the walls of co-educational universities, destroyed her chances of getting married. Within the last ten years this has changed a lot, and it is possible occasionally to see a girl who is neither a prostitute nor married walking alone with a man in a park or even sitting with him on a bench. It is still almost unknown for a young Egyptian male to take a young girl out for the evening, but in another ten years it is likely to be quite common.

Social change in Egypt's big cities, apparent to anyone revisiting the country after a few years' absence, has still only just begun to affect the villages where the great majority of the population live. Here male values are supreme, and it is virtually impossible for any girl to show independence. Crimes of honour in which a *fellah* kills his daughter, sister, or cousin because some breath of scandal has touched her are still quite common. The new schools, rural centres, radio, television and the cinema as well as the government's encouragement of political consciousness among women are bound to undermine the present system eventually, but it will take many years for it to register any basic change.

If education has hitherto done most to raise the status of Egyptian women, a change in the divorce and marriage laws would probably achieve as much more quickly. A Laws of Personal Status Committee, with a majority of senior Muslim sheikhs but including one woman lawyer and deputy, had been considering the matter for some years in the summer of 1964. Among the proposals it was contemplating, apart from raising the marriage age the need for which has already been mentioned, were: making polygamy illegal except in cases of 'necessity', i.e. where the wife is sterile or suffers from an incurable disease; making the present easy divorce more difficult by obliging any husband who wishes to divorce his wife to refer his marital difficulties to a local committee of the Arab Socialist Union, which will try to reconcile the two parties and only issue a certificate of divorce if it fails; and abolishing the so-called 'Bait al-Ta'ah' or House of Obedience law whereby a husband can summon the police to force a wife who has left him to return. Any or all of these measures would immeasurably help to improve the position of women, provided they could be effectively enforced.

The strength of parental control and family ties have so far prevented juvenile delinquency from becoming a major social problem in Egyptian towns, although it may appear with other symptoms of progress in the course of Egypt's industrial revolution. Similarly, alcoholism and drunkenness have not reached any serious proportions, partly because of the prohibition by religion and custom but perhaps even more because of the lack of cheap spirits. They are equally rare among the Christian Copts. On the other hand, the authorities have made almost no progress in limiting the use of narcotics, and especially hashish, in spite of tremendous efforts and the very severe penalties imposed on the drug traffic. Like gin in eighteenth-century Britain, hashish helps the poor Egyptian to forget the drudgery of his life, but it is also common among the middle class. The belief among Egyptian males that it adds to their sexual prowess may have something to do with this. In January 1965 a member of the National Assembly who had made a special study of the subject said that about thirty per cent of the Egyptian people smoked hashish and 20,000 were in prison on narcotics charges. He estimated the amount spent each year in Cairo alone on hashish at the astonishing figure of £E. 30 million. A psychiatrist's report found that out of 500 bus drivers investigated, seventy per cent were narcotics users, and of these eighty-eight per cent were hashish smokers with the rest opium addicts.

The regime has tackled the housing problem with energy, as the blocks of new low-rent flats outside all the towns testify. But the clearance of all the vast areas of over-crowded slums that remain will cost much more than the country can contemplate at present. City planning unfortunately takes a low priority in the rush to build factories. Nevertheless, there is a growing feeling among many Egyptians that the municipal authorities could do much more at little cost to improve public services like traffic control, drainage, electricity supply, telephones, postal services, street cleaning and lightings, and road mending in Egyptian towns. For some of these things it is less a question of improving the administration than the civic consciousness of the public, which is still regrettably low in Egypt. One of the results of the Revolution has, happily, been to make the mass of the people feel for the first time that the cities belong to them and that they can walk and sit when and where they like in streets, on the grass in public squares or along the Nile. But to welcome this is not to deny that it makes the garbage-collectors' task more difficult. Any realistic socialist will admit that a nationalized building will not be as well kept as when it was privately owned unless vigorous steps are taken to see that it is. If the Egyptian Government were to use the considerable powers it already holds to campaign against public squalor, there is little doubt that it could make Egypt's cities and towns substantially cleaner and tidier. Socialism is not necessarily synonymous with shabbiness.

One of the difficulties is the low calibre of the civil police who, except for the officers, are badly paid and come from the poorest and least educated stratum of society. Although some efforts have been made to raise their standards, the ordinary policemen still have no real authority with the public, which feels encouraged to show contempt for civic regulations.

8 Education and Culture

Most newly independent countries regard education as the key to development and progress, but none more so than Egypt. Egyptian nationalists were convinced that successive British Government representatives had deliberately stifled education and starved it of funds because they believed, quite correctly, that it would foster nationalist feelings. Between the two World Wars, therefore, when Egypt gained independence in its internal affairs, successive governments devoted a large part of their efforts to expanding the educational system. The total school population increased from 324,000 in 1913 to 942,000 in 1933 and 1,900,000 in 1951. The revolutionary regime redoubled these efforts until it was opening new schools at the rate of two every three days. Vocational schools for industry, commerce, and agriculture were immensely increased in size and number. In 1953 they had 15,000 students at the primary and secondary levels, and they now have over 100,000.

By 1961 the school population was 3.5 million and today it is approaching four million. The number of university students rose from 38,000 in 1951 to 53,000 in 1961. A new university was opened at Assiut in 1957 while the ancient Islamic University of al-Azhar was partially transformed into a modern university in 1961 by the addition of science, medical, and engineering faculties. Meanwhile the number of foreign students studying in Egypt rose from 3,200 in 1952 to 18,845 in 1962, a demand on facilities only in part offset by an increase in the number of Egyptians studying abroad from 1,984 to 5,575 in the same period. The Ministry of Education's budget has risen from £E. 1,600,000 in 1920 to £E. 40.2 million in 1951 and £E. 96.5 million in 1964.

There are now school vacancies for about eighty per cent of

the population attaining the age of six, and since the annual rate of expansion is about ten per cent the goal of providing primary education for the entire population is well within sight.

Primary education from the age of six to twelve is in fact free and compulsory by law, and the government is determined to make this a reality. However, the figures for school enrolment do not give the whole picture. In the towns attendance in primary schools is normally about eighty-five per cent of the enrolment, while in the country it drops to sixty per cent or lower in the summer when children are needed to work in the cotton fields. At the secondary level attendance is higher at about ninety-six per cent of enrolment. But as in every other field, the government has to tackle the basic economic problems along with the social ones. Any law forbidding the use of child labour so as to ensure school attendance will be quite unenforceable as long as the *fellahin* need their children to search for the cotton leaf worm.

The actual physical expansion of educational opportunities in Egypt since the Revolution has been very impressive, and the government is quite right in thinking that education is the prerequisite for progress in everything else. The question is whether the increase in quantity would have been possible without the decline in quality that has undoubtedly taken place at the same time.

Some of the criticisms that are levelled against the educational policy of the revolutionary regime show no understanding of the motives behind it. Before the Revolution, 300 foreign schools produced a social and cultural élite in Egypt. The standards at these schools were often the same as those of the best in Europe, but so also were the ideas and assumptions on which their teaching was based. Egyptian boys and girls who went there frequently could neither read nor write Arabic and prided themselves on not being able to do so. They felt no sympathy for the great mass of their fellow countrymen, and it is not surprising that the revolutionary regime regarded such schools as a breeding-ground for one of Egypt's worst social evils, its irresponsible aristocracy. During the past ten years the foreign schools have all either been nationalized or put under close

State control and forced to change their curricula to conform with the State system.

In removing Egypt's former cultural aristocracy from power the regime is also trying to push through a technical and economic revolution. Egypt's new élite is composed of scientists, doctors, engineers, architects, factory managers and army officers. In the universities the brightest students generally take medical or engineering degrees, while the less promising study the arts. Professors in the arts faculties unanimously complain of a disastrous drop in standards which is due, at least in part, to a change in the cultural climate of the country. Anyone who mixed with the witty, cosmopolitan, self-confident members of the pre-revolutionary Egyptian cultural élite is likely to find their successors philistine, serious, and dull. But they have a much better understanding of their country's needs.

When all the allowances have been made, however, the present state of Egyptian education should be a cause of grave concern to the government. In its early days the regime undertook to provide free education for all citizens and has made a determined effort to do this which is within sight of succeeding. But owing to the breakneck speed of expansion, classes are far too large at all levels, while many of the teachers are quite unqualified for their jobs. Moreover, the shortage of teachers is made much worse by the export of many to other Arab countries; in 1964 there were about 5,000 in Algeria, Yemen, Saudi Arabia and elsewhere. Cases are recorded of children who after six years primary education are still illiterate; far too much learning is memorized undigested. Examinations, which are all-important in the Egyptian system, are rigid and unimaginative; in 1964, for instance, every student was certain that there would be a question on the High Dam and memorized the facts accordingly. These were all faults of the pre-revolutionary system also, but they have certainly become worse.

There are strong arguments for the 'Egyptianization' and Arabization' of the Egyptian educational system. The question of whether medicine and the natural sciences should or should not be taught in Arabic is one on which Egyptian doctors and scientists themselves disagree, but it does not affect the general principle. Any revolutionary regime dedicated to ending class privilege within Egypt and political influence from outside was bound to modify the pre-revolutionary educational system radically through various forms of 'nationalization'. The trouble is that in doing so it has imposed a stifling uniformity which suppresses, or at least fails to encourage, the initiative of the brighter and more original pupils who are the leaven of the whole system.

There has been a parallel effect on the teachers. In the universities some of the outstanding lecturers were either imprisoned for their opinions or forced to avoid saying anything provocative. Most of them were leftish rather than *ancien régime* in their views (although quite often they were both) and they suffered most during the anti-Communist drive of 1959–61. Denunciations by students were sometimes acted upon by the secret police. However, there were several signs of an improvement in the atmosphere in late 1963 and 1964.

The rigid discipline of the regime does have one advantage. In the years immediately preceding the Revolution secondary and university students spent so much time in political demonstrations that they had little left over for study. Since the Revolution, students have been forbidden to demonstrate except on rare occasions, such as after the murder of Lumumba, when they were encouraged by the authorities.

There are good prospects that at least some of the deficiencies can be remedied in the future. If the present rate of expansion is maintained, once primary schools are provided for the whole population some of the effort and investment can be devoted to reducing the size of the classes and to teacher training. Some Egyptian educationalists draw a parallel with the Soviet Union, which concentrated in the early years after the revolution on combating illiteracy and providing schools for all children. This led to some of the same faults as mark the present Egyptian system, but today Soviet education is acknowledged to be as good in many respects as that of the most advanced Western nations. Moreover, despite the heavily nationalist atmosphere in present-day Egypt, it is nothing like as xenophobic as it was in Stalinist Russia. If the import of foreign books, periodicals, and films is strictly limited, the reason for this is almost entirely the shortage of foreign exchange.

There is a parallel trend to the educational system in Egypt's cultural life, which is becoming at once more widespread, popular, and indigenous in character. The government regards culture as a vitally important aspect of Egypt's nationalist and socialist revolution. It has spent and is spending very heavily on radio, television, the theatre, cinema, and the arts, with the mixed motives of raising the cultural level of the masses, increasing Egypt's prestige, and disseminating propaganda. With radio, the propaganda motive is predominant, and expansion has been phenomenal. The thirty-three hours of daily broadcasting in 1952 had been increased to 394 in 1964. At home there are four programmes – the general, the 'Voice of the Arabs', one called 'With the People' and the European service in a variety of European languages – while since 1953 external programmes have been beamed to Asia, Africa, Europe, and the Americas in twenty different languages.

Egyptian television was inaugurated in 1960 and is now much more highly developed than in any other Arab State, with three channels active for a total of twenty-eight hours a day. It covers most of the country except for Upper Egypt between Kom-Ombo and Assiut, and this gap will be closed soon. In 1964 there were about 300,000 sets in the country or nearly twelve per 1,000 inhabitants. This is still low, but the number of sets is increasing by about 100,000 a year, and demand for the locally assembled sets always exceeds supply. In 1964 the television factories were producing 300 sets a day, with about seventy per cent of the manufacturing operation carried out in Egypt.

While rather fewer foreign theatre companies come to perform at the Cairo Opera than they used to before the Revolution, the Egyptian theatre is itself enjoying a boom. In the winter of 1963–4 there were nine or ten theatres in Cairo performing classical and modern Arabic plays, some Egyptian operettas and comedies, and also translations of foreign plays ranging from Shakespeare through Chekhov to Ionesco. Those who are able to compare the Cairo theatre today with the 1920s and

1930s say that production, décor, and acting have all much improved. Arabs generally have a strong aversion to Western opera, but brave attempts to produce *The Merry Widow*, *La Traviata*, and Benjamin Britten's *Let's Make an Opera* in Arabic have met with considerable public success.

Television has also been a stimulus to actors and producers – although, as elsewhere, the complaint is often heard that it draws talent and money away from the real theatre. There are two television ballet troupes which frequently perform in Cairo theatres. There is also the now famous Reda folk-dancing troupe which has made several world tours. Because traditional Egyptian folk-dancing hardly exists, it has had to be invented, but the result is excellent entertainment.

The Egyptian cinema industry is the only one of any consequence in the Arab States and is among the twelve biggest in the world. In 1964 work was started on the construction of a great 'Cinema City' on a 50-acre site outside Cairo, and at about the same time several contracts were signed for films to be co-produced with Italian, German, and American companies. At present Egypt is producing fifty to sixty feature films a year and recently has begun to compete at international film festivals. It must be admitted, however, that very few of these show any real quality and most are outstandingly bad. The cinema is in fact nationalized, but the fault does not lie with any deadening State control; the trouble is rather that the Egyptian cinema has never managed to abandon the techniques and clichés of thirty years ago. Melodrama takes the place of tension and excitement, while farce makes do for comedy. Modern Egypt cries out for realistic treatment by the cinema, but this has scarcely yet been tried.

Dr Hatem, Deputy Prime Minister for Culture and National Guidance, is determined to nourish popular culture and provide entertainment for the mass of the people particularly in the country and provincial towns. He plans to build more theatres outside Cairo and 4,000 cinemas all over the country to cover every village of any size. Together with television this will do much to lighten the dreariness of Egyptian provincial and country life.

The state is heavily subsidizing the arts in several other ways. Young Egyptian painters receive scholarships which alone enable them to continue painting since there are very few private buyers of pictures in modern Egypt. Outside Cairo a 'City of Arts' includes a ballet school (with a staff of Soviet teachers), a music school (teaching both Arabic and Western music), a cinema school and a theatre school, in all of which tuition is free. All this can scarcely be criticized. Whatever the arguments may be against state subsidization of the arts, the fact is that in modern Egypt they could hardly survive at all without government support. Doubts have been expressed over whether Egypt can afford this expenditure, but it is probable that the country makes a handsome profit through the sale of films and television programmes to other Arab States and through maintaining Cairo as the cultural and entertainment centre of the Arab world. (Beirut rivals Cairo in some respects, especially Arabic book publishing, but it is too cosmopolitan ever to be a major centre of Arab culture. Its cabarets and night-clubs are better than Cairo's, but they are Western not Arab.)

Nevertheless, the State's near monopoly of culture and entertainment does have serious drawbacks. The element of propaganda which penetrates every sphere of education and the arts has already been mentioned. It has now become so much a part of Egyptian life that young people take it for granted and fail to notice its presence. Because Egypt's achievements in the arts are so bound up with its national prestige, there is almost no serious criticism, though this is what Egyptian artists need most. There are a number of talented Egyptian painters (although most of these are decorative and lacking in depth) and there are also some very bad ones. The rare art criticism to appear in the national Press praises them all equally, which is bad for both categories. It may be argued that in some branches of the arts to which attention in Egypt is just beginning to be given, such as classical ballet, encouragement and protection are needed to foster the infant; but in most of the arts Egypt should by now have come of age. Cinema directors and script-writers, for instance, who consistently underestimate the intelligence of their audience could well be made to submit to the kind of savage criticism that appears in the London weekly Press.

The Egyptian Press itself suffers from similar handicaps. It was perhaps inevitable that the revolutionary government should not permit the sort of cynical satire of its activities for which the Cairo Press used to be famous. Criticism and abuse is now all directed abroad at foreign governments and personalities who of course cannot answer back in any way which will reach Egyptian newspaper readers. Consequently Egyptian journalists can be as tendentious and inaccurate as they please in their reporting and comment on foreign affairs without fear of contradiction. In writing of home affairs, on the other hand, they find it difficult to avoid being pompous and dull. Most Egyptians have a fine nihilistic sense of humour which is still very much alive. Today it finds its outlet in a series of political jokes about the regime which, according to legend, President Nasser enjoys hearing during his brief moments of leisure. What the Egyptian Press has not yet been able to achieve is a synthesis between this type of humour and a serious approach to politics so as to produce the kind of balanced, informal yet essentially readable article which can be found in the world's free Presses.

It would not be fair to say that the Egyptian Press is rigidly State-controlled. It has much more freedom than the Press of Eastern Europe, for instance, even in this post-Stalinist era. Dr Hatem was no doubt sincere when he told the National Assembly in June 1964 that there was no government control of the Press at all. But it is difficult to believe that he would tolerate in the newspapers a sharp detailed criticism of the policies of his Ministry such as several well-known Egyptian journalists express in private. The inescapable conclusion is that what the Egyptian Press lacks most is moral courage.

In the summer of 1964 the limited but genuine relaxation in the political atmosphere which followed the abolition of emergency regulations and the election of the National Assembly provided an opportunity for the Cairo Press to show more spirit and independence. Whether it did nor not depended to a large extent on a few men at the top of the profession such as

Muhammad Hasanein Heykal, the editor of *al-Ahram*; Ahmed Bahai ed-Din, who early in 1964 left his job as chief political commentator on the weekly *Akhbar el-Yaum* (Egypt's closest equivalent to London's *Sunday Express* in style and tone) to direct the big Dal el-Hillal publishing house; and the left-wing Khaled Muhieddin, who returned to public life in 1964 as chairman of the board of *Akhbar* newspapers.

As a close friend of President Nasser, Heykal is as near to the centre of power as any newspaper proprietor might wish, and his Friday editorials are usually read as expressions of the Egyptian Government's thoughts. But this role of semi-official spokesman for Egypt also means that neither he nor his paper (which is now well ahead of its two rival dailies, *al-Akhbar* and *al-Goumhouriyah*, in circulation) can act as a truly independent critic.

Ahmed Bahai ed-Din is a political journalist of high calibre. When he took over Dar el-Hillal he made an immediate impression by making its illustrated weekly magazine *al-Musawar* both more thoughtful and more stimulating.

Khaled Muhieddin, who also holds the position of Chairman of the Arab Socialist Union Press Committee, has set himself the task of interpreting Egypt's new political system to his readers, but it remains uncertain whether he enjoys anything like the close confidential relations with President Nasser which is the chief source of Heykal's influence.

9 Economic Policies

Like most army revolutionaries, the Free Officers had nothing resembling a comprehensive programme for economic reform when they came to power in 1952. A few of them, such as Khaled Muhieddin, had absorbed some Marxist ideas, but none of them had thought out how these should be applied to Egypt. The only radical measure that they were agreed was necessary was agrarian reform, but even the details of this had to be urgently worked out during the first few weeks after the Revolution. Land reform was at that stage essentially a political measure; while it had an important socio-economic aspect in its aim to improve the lot of the *fellahin* through reducing rents for agricultural land, its chief purpose was to break the political power of the big landowners who had successfully blocked reform for generations.

The economic policies of Nasser's Egypt have evolved over the past twelve years, with external circumstances deciding the pace but not the direction in which they have moved. Nasser's reading of Egyptian history and his basic political aim of a renascent, self-reliant Egypt, freed from all forms of foreign domination and playing a key role in the Arab world and Africa, made it virtually inevitable that sooner or later he would seek solutions in a crash programme of industrialization and a highly centralized, nationalistic socialism. Suez gave a sharp impetus to the process of removing foreign economic influence and also turned Egypt away from its traditional trading partners in the West towards the Eastern bloc. Syria's secession from the U.A.R. in 1961 gave Nasser a jerk to the left because he believed that it had been engineered by the capitalist classes in Syria, with sympathetic support from their Egyptian counterparts, against the extension of U.A.R. socialism. But without Suez or the secession, the trend would have been the same.

In the early years after the Revolution Nasser's thoughts and energies were heavily absorbed by foreign affairs. Between 1958 and 1961 it was the problems of union with Syria which took up most of his time. The secession therefore gave him the opportunity to think out his ideas on Egypt's social, political and economic structure and the result is contained in the National Charter, a 30,000-word document which he presented to the National Congress of Popular Powers on 21 May 1962. Much of this consists of his explanations of the need for fundamental social revolution in Egypt and, as might be expected, it is coloured throughout with his sense of Egypt's own history. Most of the practical proposals have already been put into effect, and it seems likely that as long as Nasser's authority inside Egypt remains without serious challenge, the system he has evolved will survive with only minor changes.

The essence of his economic argument can be found in a passage where he considers the reasons for the failure of Saad Zaghloul's 1919 revolution.

The leaders of the 1919 revolution could not see clearly that a revolution cannot achieve its aims for the people unless it goes beyond the mere political goal of independence and tackles the roots of economic and social problems. The most that could be done at that time was to demand that some financial activities be Egyptianized whereas there was a more pressing need for a radical redistribution of wealth.

This failure to carry through a social revolution in the 1920s enabled imperialism to maintain its influence after independence.

'It paved the way for a batch of capitalists, who in fact inherited the role of the nineteenth-century foreign adventurers who made only a superficial impression and failed to develop the country.' These capitalists, like the politicians and intellectuals, 'all fell into the arms of the palace at one time and of imperialism at another'.

From this he concludes that

in the countries forced to remain under-developed, a free capitalist system is no longer able to lead the economic drive at a time when the great capitalist monopolies in the advanced developed countries can rely on the exploitation of the sources of wealth in the colonies. Local capitalism can only survive either by tariff protection, which is paid for by the mass of the people, or by making itself an appendage to world monopolies and dooming the country to subservience.

The race to catch up with the developed countries cannot be left to 'desultory individual efforts motivated by private profit'.

Three steps must accordingly be taken: mobilization of national savings; the use of modern scientific techniques to exploit these savings; and the drafting of a complete plan for production.

The absence of a social revolution, runs Nasser's argument, also meant that Egyptian parliamentary democracy before the revolution was a sham.

Political democracy cannot be separated from social democracy. No citizen can be regarded as free to vote unless he is given the following three guarantees: (a) he should be free from exploitation in all its forms; (b) he should enjoy an equal opportunity with his fellow citizens to enjoy a fair share of the national wealth; (c) his mind should be free from all anxiety likely to undermine his future security.

Thus, in Nasser's view, neither national independence, nor true democracy, nor the status of an economically developed country can be achieved without socialism. He summarizes the economic aspect of socialism in Egypt as:

First – That the economic infrastructure including railways, roads, ports, airports, power supplies, dams, sea, land and air transport, and other public services should all come under public ownership.

Second – The majority of heavy, medium, and mining industries should be publicly owned. Although it is possible to allow private ownership in this field, it should be controlled by the public sector owned by the people. Light industries must be free from monopoly, and though this field is open to private enterprise it must be guided by the public sector.

Third – Foreign trade must be under the people's full control. All the import trade must be within the public sector, and although private capital has a part to play in the export trade, the public sector must possess the main share so as to prevent all possibilities of fraudulence. If the proportion is to be fixed exactly, the public sector must control three-quarters of exports while the private sector is responsible for the rest. The public sector must within the coming eight years take charge of at least one quarter of domestic trade to prevent monopoly, and expand the range of internal trade before private and cooperative activities.

Fourth – Banks and insurance companies should come under the public sector to ensure that capital is not left a purely speculative role, to protect national savings and to ensure against their misdirection.

Fifth – There must be a clear distinction between the exploiting and non-exploiting ownership of land. Agricultural land is limited to one hundred *feddans* per family. The ownership of buildings is controlled by taxation and rent restriction. Constant supervision is still essential to prevent exploitation, but the increase in public and cooperative housing will assist in this matter.

As the basis of an economic programme this gives the State a bigger role than merely 'occupying the commanding heights of the economy', as the British Labour Party phrases the socialist objective today, but it leaves more to the private sector than Marxism. The Marxist influence on Nasser's historical analysis of Egypt's 'failed revolutions' in the 1880s and 1919 is obvious. There is also a strong element of Titoism in his views on the structure of the Egyptian State. But whatever the outside influences he has absorbed, his conclusions have a strongly Egyptian flavour which is wholly to be expected from such a devoted nationalist. As he remarks: 'The real solutions to the problems of the people cannot be derived from the experiences of another.'

Several important differences from orthodox Marxism in his political creed have been emphasized by Nasser himself. He rejects, for instance, such ideas as the atheistic State and the dictatorship of the proletariat. In the economic sphere, he proclaims that the production of consumer goods should not be neglected through the concentration on heavy industry.

Heavy industry no doubt provides the solid foundation for any large-scale industrial framework ... but the masses of our people have been long deprived; to mobilize all of them for the building of heavy industry and overlook their needs as consumers is incompatible with their right to make up for their long deprivation and delays. ...

This idea that the mass of the Egyptian people deserve to be compensated for their past sufferings colours all Nasser's thinking. It is the reason for the continuation of subsidies for basic necessities despite Egypt's present acute economic difficulties, which are partly due to a massive rise in consumption in the towns and cities. Nasser would passionately discard any scheme that allowed prices to rise as a means of reducing consumption.

As has been said above, the economic principles of the regime took several years to evolve. In fact the policies of the early years after the Revolution were more liberal and orthodox than before. When the Free Officers took over, the country was tottering into bankruptcy as a result of the irresponsible actions of the last Wafd government; there were heavy deficits in the budget and the balance of payments in both 1951 and 1952. The new Finance Minister, Dr Abdel Galil al-Emary, pushed through a drastic policy of deflation and austerity through import and currency restrictions and severe cuts in government expenditures. Imports were reduced from £E. 210.5 million to £E. 150.7 million in 1954, and the balance of payments actually showed a surplus of £E. 3.3 million in 1954.

Similarly, the budget deficit was turned into a surplus of £E. 6.7 million in 1953–4. There was no attempt at central planning but two new bodies were created, the Permanent Council for Social Services and the Permanent Council for the Development of National Production, composed of technicians and economists with the task of studying and reporting on all schemes presented by the various Ministries. As research and advisory bodies these did valuable work, but their scope was necessarily limited. The Finance Ministry set out to attract private Egyptian and foreign capital into investment in Egyptian industry and other socially profitable enterprises. Hopes that after the agrarian reform the large landowners would invest their capital in industry were soon disappointed, however, for they diverted it into real estate. Attempts to attract foreign capital were equally unsuccessful. In an effort to reassure foreign investors, some pre-revolutionary legislation of nationalist character was amended; Law No. 138 of 1947, which required all foreign limited companies in Egypt to have at least fifty-one per cent of Egyptian capital, was amended so as to reduce the minimum to forty-nine per cent. But the part of Law 147 stipulating that ninety per cent of the workers in foreign companies should be Egyptian and receive eighty per cent of the salaries, was retained. Foreign capital remained extremely wary of the young military regime.

By the end of 1954 the government had come to realize that it would have to increase expenditure even if it meant deficit financing. There was an urgent need to step up the pace of development because production was failing to keep up with the growth of population. Although even reasonably accurate estimates for *per capita* income are unavailable, it seems virtually certain that this was falling between 1952 and 1954. At the same time the new military regime wished to increase expenditure on defence and on health, education, and other social services to satisfy the popular hopes that had been raised by the Revolution. Public expenditure increased from £E. 233 million in 1953–4 to £E. 358.1 million in 1956–7. Of this only about five per cent was government investment in development, and the rest was current expenditure. A separate Development Budget was created which was financed mainly through public loans and the banks and by foreign loans and aid; it is estimated that the proportion of outstanding public debt to national income rose from 22.4 per cent in 1954 to 28.6 per cent in 1957.

Orthodox conservative economic policies had been thrown out of the window, but Egypt was still a long way from socialism. Even by 1959–60 only eighteen per cent of the Gross Domestic Product originated in the public sector, compared with sixteen per cent at the Revolution, and only twelve per cent of the labour force was employed by the government. Subsidies for basic necessities were used to keep down the cost of living for the mass of the people, but at the same time the government kept much stricter control over the trade-unions than before the Revolution and strikes were prohibited. Any European socialist would probably have described the system as 'State-controlled capitalism'.

The Suez war in 1956 had several important effects on the economic scene. Domestic prices rose sharply, and there was a drastic fall in the price of the Egyptian pound abroad; an economic boycott by the West (including the U.S.A.) and the consequent loss of export markets caused a severe strain on the balance of payments. Net holdings of foreign assets were reduced from £E. 214 million in 1954 to £E. 110.6 million in 1957. The Egyptian economy was saved from disaster by the Communist bloc countries, several of which concluded bilateral trade agreements with Egypt; but these did not altogether compensate for the loss of Western markets, especially because the Eastern European countries resold some of the cotton they had taken from Egypt in Western Europe at a discount.

The Egyptian Government's immediate response to the Anglo-French invasion was to sequester all British and French property. A series of laws issued in January 1957 obliged all foreign banks and insurance companies to Egyptianize themselves, and British and French banks, such as Barclay's and Crédit Lyonnais, were sold to Egyptian banks. Together with the nationalization of the Suez Canal company, this meant that the greater part of the foreign share in the Egyptian economy had been liquidated. Much of this share was transferred to the Egyptian Government, and between 1957 and 1960 a number of public economic organizations were created, while others already in existence were expanded, to look after the government's interests and to fill the vacuum left by Egyptian private capital; these included the Economic Development Organization, the Bank Misr, the General Organization for Maritime Transportation, the al-Nasr Organization, and the Suez Canal Authority. At the end of 1959 the total assets of the various companies affiliated to the Economic Development Organization amounted to some £E. 506 million, of which more than half was in banking and one quarter in industry, mining, and agriculture.

The State's actual share in the economy was growing, and a trend had begun which ensured that it would continue to do so. The 1956 republican constitution stated that 'development must be planned'. A State National Planning Committee was established which absorbed the semi-private Permanent Council for the Development of National Production, and in 1958 a Five-Year Plan for Industry was launched in which the State was to provide sixty-one per cent of the finance – mainly for the heavy industry programme. Thus although only eighteen per cent of the Gross Domestic Product originated in the public sector by 1959–60, seventy-four per cent of total investment was undertaken by the government compared with only thirty-one per cent in 1952–8. If the trend continued, the industrial sector of the Egyptian economy would inevitably become socialized, although it would be a long time before the State actually held a majority share. Towards the end of 1957 Nasser first spoke of a 'socialist, democratic, cooperative system' as Egypt's goal. But the State's role was still strictly limited. On 5 December 1957 he told the Cooperatives Conference at Cairo University:

In dealing with feudalism our aim was to transform tenants into owners. Thus we shall have a socialist, democratic, cooperative society. When the State intervenes in industry it does not mean at all that it is the only capitalist. We believe that national capitalism is essential to strengthen and expand our economy and to achieve our country's economic independence.

In February 1958 Egypt entered into the union with Syria which

called for a period of adjustment. Egypt was already far ahead in building a socialist pattern of a planned economy with a land reform, a large public sector, an industrial five-year plan and highly progressive taxation. Syria had a private enterprise mercantile economy with minimum controls on imports and foreign exchange. (National Bank of Egypt, Economic Bulletin, Vol. XVII, No. 1.)

Throughout 1958 and most of 1959 Nasser was deeply involved in trying to create a workable political structure for the union and had in addition to deal with urgent problems of foreign policy raised by the anti-government insurrection in Lebanon, the Iraqi revolution followed by the landing of American troops in Lebanon and British troops in Jordan, and in early 1959 by his breach with General Kassem and his near-break with the Soviet Union. Except for one or two occasions such as the inauguration of the Iron and Steel Plant at Helwan, Nasser's speeches were devoted exclusively to foreign affairs and Arab nationalism. For the time being the 'socialist, democratic, cooperative society' was scarcely mentioned.

By the end of 1959 Egypt, Nasser, and his able Finance Minister, Dr Abdul Moneim el-Kaissouny, were ready for a new move towards socialism, but this time they were going to take a deeply reluctant Syria at least part of the way with them. In Egypt the move began in February 1960 with the nationalization of the Bank Misr and the National Bank of Egypt.

'The step was significant because the previous 1956 nationalizations had been concerned with foreign-owned firms while this was concerned with firms owned or mainly owned by nationals.' (National Bank of Egypt, Economic Bulletin, Vol. XVII, No. 1.)

In June 1960 the Press was nationalized, and the Cairo bus services were municipalized. But the really big step was taken in June and July 1961. In a series of decrees the government took over the entire import trade of the country and a large part of the export trade including cotton, which is much the biggest item in Egypt's exports. All banks and insurance companies were nationalized, and about 300 industrial and trading establishments were taken over either wholly or partly by the State. A highly progressive taxation system was introduced with the declared objective of making £E. 5,000 a year the maximum income in Egypt. Individual shareholdings in companies affected by the July nationalization decrees were limited to £E. 10,000. The working day in industry was limited to seven hours (as a means of increasing employment), and a quarter of all profits made by companies was to be distributed to the workers.

In July 1960 a comprehensive Five-Year Plan for 1960–5 was launched. This was to be followed by a second Five-Year Plan for 1965–70 with the target of doubling the national income by 1970. The 1958 Five-Year Plan for Industry, which had already had considerable success in speeding up industrialization, especially in light industry, was absorbed into the new Five-Year Plan, which now covered the agricultural sector as well. This time eighty per cent of the £E. 1,634 million to be invested would be undertaken by the public sector. About forty per cent would be allocated to industry and twenty-five per cent to increasing the agricultural potential.

Some of the socialist decrees were also applied to the Syrian region. The Five-Year Plan for Syria put the government's share of the total investment at fifty-six per cent, which was not as high as Egypt's eighty per cent but still a substantial increase on the nineteen per cent provided by the Syrian public sector as the proportion of total investment in 1954–6. Before the union with Egypt, the Syrian economic system had been predominantly *laissez-faire* capitalist, and there was a powerful and experienced business and merchant class that bitterly opposed the progress towards socialism. When part of the Syrian army rebelled against the union in August 1961, this class immediately supported the secession.

It was a terrible blow to Nasser's prestige which many thought might be mortal. In his bitter self-criticism after the secession, he declared:

We fell victims to a dangerous illusion. . . . We always refused to make peace with imperialism, but we made the mistake of making peace with reaction. . . . Closely connected with this illusion is another illusion, that it is possible to reach a compromise with reaction on national grounds. . . . We have seen how Syria, capitalism, feudalism and opportunism joined forces with imperialism to wipe out the gains of the masses and to strike at the socialist revolution.

His conclusion was that the capitalist and land-owning classes had taken their revenge. They had managed to infiltrate into the National Union, the U.A.R.'s single political organization created after the union, and now that they had had their way in Syria there was a grave danger that they would try to do the same in Egypt. There was a story going around Cairo that a toast had been drunk to Syria's secession at the bar of the Gezira Club, still a focal point for the unreconciled old regime.

The precautionary counter-offensive took place in Egypt between October 1961 and February 1962. Six hundred of Egypt's wealthiest families, a high proportion of them Copts and Jews, had their property sequestered by the State. About forty were arrested, and although they were released three or four months later, all of them and those affected by the sequestration were politically 'isolated', forbidden to vote or take part in the political life of the State.

These sequestrations hardly added up to the 'liquidation of the Egyptian kulaks' as they were described in the Beirut Press. Compared with the nationalizations and the July decrees, they were of minor political or economic importance. But they received very bad publicity abroad, because it looked as if the regime in its rage at not being able to harm the Syrian bourgeoisie had turned on its own. Some of the best known figures among those who had been sequestered, such as the multimillionaire industrialists Ahmed Abboud and Francois Tagher, were known to have been encouraged by the regime until very recently to expand their investments, on the understanding that they were regarded as patriotic national capitalists and would not be touched. The large number of non-Muslims among the sequestered also gave the impression of religious discrimination; certainly it would be difficult to deny that some bias was shown against the minorities, but it is also true that any comprehensive list of Egyptian millionaires would have included a high proportion of Copts, Jews and Levantines.

In August 1963 there was a further series of nationalizations covering some firms which had already been partly nationalized, some companies in part privately owned under sequestration, and private companies. About 300 concerns were affected including the Dutch-British Lever Brothers, fourteen partly nationalized shipping companies, and twenty-nine land transport companies. At the same time under Republican Decree 73 all contracts for quarrying and mining issued to private concerns were ended.

The model for the economic structure of the country presented by President Nasser in the National Charter was now virtually complete, and private enterprise had been relegated to a relatively minor role. In the phrase of the Egyptian Marxist Anwar Abdul Malek the 'dismantling of the Old Bourgeoisie' had been achieved. Private property had not been abolished, but as a result of the land reform and nationalizations there had been a redistribution of the national wealth; as Mr Aly Sabry, the Minister of Presidential Affairs, said after the issuing of the July decrees: 'The public sector is not for us a means of liquidating property but of spreading it wider.' On the other hand, large-scale investment by private Egyptian *entrepreneurs* had been effectively discouraged. None of the capitalists who had been left at large could be sure that his concerns would not suddenly be taken over by the State, however well regarded by the regime he might feel he was at present. There was therefore good reason to believe that even the minor twenty per cent share of investment in the first Five-Year Plan that had been allocated to private enterprise was too optimistic.

After the 1963 nationalizations Mr Aly Sabry more than once gave assurances that private buildings were not going to be nationalized, and in March 1964 when the new provisional constitution was introduced it was announced that all sequestrations were to be wound up. Each sequestered person would be allowed to keep property or shares up to a value of £E. 30,000 in addition to all furniture or jewels or other valuables that had been kept at home.

In 1964 it seemed unlikely that the government intended to sequester or nationalize any further on a substantial scale, although efforts to rationalize the structure of industry might involve taking over small firms to merge them into larger groups. This in fact was done in March 1964 to 119 contracting companies – already fifty per cent nationalized by the 1961 decrees – which were fully nationalized and merged into thirty-five companies.

But the attitude of private investors both outside and inside the country remained cautious and suspicious with good reason. In April 1964 there was a laconic government announcement that Shell–BP interests in the U.A.R. had been nationalized. Since Esso and Mobiloil were not touched it seemed likely that there was a political motive behind the move; Anglo-Egyptian relations were at a low ebb because of the situation in South Arabia. In 1963 two U.S. companies had entered into partnership arrangements with the Egyptian Petroleum Organization for oil exploration in the country, and at the time the Minister of Industry Dr Aziz Sidqi had said, in an interview published in *Petroleum Intelligence Weekly* on 25 November, that among the advantages to foreign concessionaires of signing agreements with Egypt were: the political stability of the government; the 100 per cent certainty that the contract would be respected; and the clear definition of policy by the Egyptian Government which left the concessionaire in no doubt where he stood. There was some truth in these claims, and it certainly seemed highly improbable that Egypt would break any new contract entered into after the nationalization decrees. But the Shell nationalization (like the sequestration of Belgian property in Egypt during the Congo crisis of 1960) emphasized the fact that Egypt's economic policies were influenced by political events. It was always conceivable that a sudden deterioration in the relations between Egypt and the U.S. would cause the Egyptian Government to revise its attitude towards American interests in the country.

There was also the problem of compensation. In 1938, when the Mexican Government nationalized all the oil companies in Mexico, the U.S. Government publicly acknowledged the right of a sovereign State to nationalize foreign-owned interests on its territory provided that adequate compensation was paid. Egypt had earned some international credit by completing the payment of compensation to the Suez Canal Company shareholders one year early; but for British, French, Belgian, Swiss, Lebanese and other interests which had been sequestered or nationalized, compensation arrangements were long delayed by lashings of red tape. In September 1964 the President of the International Bank for Reconstruction and Development, George Woods, publicly stated that the Bank would not make loans 'to countries where there had been sequestration of property without compensation within reasonable time'. There was good reason to believe that the statement was provoked by an article in *al-Ahram* on 7 August by Muhammad Hasanein Heykal in which he argued that Egypt was not morally bound to pay compensation to foreigners who had looted its wealth and that if anything the compensation should go to the Egyptian people who had been exploited. In particular he protested against an agreement which was about to be signed with the Lebanese Government and which would include the payment of nearly £E. 1 million to Francois Tagher – a man, he said, who had come penniless to Egypt at the beginning of the Second World War and had made more than £E. 4 million on the cotton market within a few years. Heykal quoted Egypt's former Finance Minister Abdul Galil al-Emary as comparing the Egyptian economy with a huge cow that grazed on Egyptian pastures but had its udders outside being milked in foreign lands.

There was much force in Heykal's argument that Egypt had been exploited in the past. But his suggestion that this freed Egypt from the moral obligation to pay adequate compensation was certain to provoke reactions like that of Mr Woods at a time when the country needed all the foreign loans it could get. On the other hand, a little-publicized agreement concluded between the United States and Egyptian Governments in 1963 whereby the U.S. Government became the ultimate guarantor of all private investments in Egypt did much to make the country more attractive to U.S. investors.

Many of the same considerations apply to Egyptian investors who have been demoralized by the series of nationalizations and sequestrations since 1960. In 1964 it would have required courage to the point of rashness for any of the remaining private companies to undertake any important new investment. Indeed the share of the private sector in total annual investment fell from 17.3 per cent in 1961–2 to 9.7 per cent in 1962–3 and then to 6.3 per cent in 1963–4. In 1963–4, 35.7 per cent of private investment was in housing, 15.1 per cent in agriculture, 7.9 per cent in irrigation and 12.6 per cent in industry. Private enterprise was playing a negligible part in the development of the Egyptian economy.

The problem was how to establish clearly the boundaries between the private and public sectors, for until this was done private *entrepreneurs* would be unlikely to take any risks. That India has been fairly successful in demarcating these boundaries shows that it can be done. One aspect of the problem was brought to the fore by President Nasser himself in his speech at the opening of the National Assembly's autumn session on 12 November 1964, when he said:

Some sectors of the government consider they have an exclusive right in the field of national action. But the National Charter stipulates that twenty-five per cent of domestic trade should be handled by the public sector and seventy-five per cent by the private sector. The provisions of the National Charter must be respected. . . . The object of forming consumers' cooperative societies is to prevent a sharp rise in prices, but if these societies monopolize home trade corruption is bound to occur in them.

Later the Minister of Supply, Dr Stino, produced figures to show that at least seventy-five per cent of domestic trade was in fact still in private hands. But there was no doubt that there had been unfair discrimination against private retailers. Consignments of imported cheese, for instance, had all been going to the cooperatives.

The two Five-Year Plans are extremely ambitious; their aim is to double the national income in ten years, with a rise of forty per cent in the first five. The targets for the various sectors are as follows (1959–60 = 100):

	1964–5	1969–70*
Heavy Industry	310	445
Light Industry	137	185
Services	128	213
Commerce	128	196
Transport, housing, public utilities, security and defence	122	160
Agriculture	128	159

*Government of the U.A.R., Five-Year Plan, Cairo, U.A.R.

The first of the Five-Year Plans assumes an overall ratio of capital invested to output of 3:1, which is low but not impossible. Similarly, the compound rate of growth for the Gross National Product is estimated at 7.2 per cent, which is high but not unattainable.

In his *Egypt in Revolution*, Charles Issawi makes some severe criticisms of the assumptions on which the Plan is based. He says:

First, the overall objectives set are often unrealistic. Secondly, there is a dearth of the basic data without which no reasonable programme, much less an overall plan, can be constructed: capital–output ratios, propensities to save, consume and import, income and price elasticities of demand and supply, technical coefficients, etc., not to mention even simpler and more fundamental data on income distribution, savings, investment and manpower resources.

Professor Issawi points out correctly that the target of doubling the national income was set first by the government and that the

Plans were made to fit it. President Nasser confirmed that this was so in his speech to the National Assembly on 12 November 1964, when he announced that the 'technicians and planners' had said the national income could be doubled in twenty years. The government had insisted on ten years. The planners had come down to eighteen, and then fifteen; but the government had stuck to ten. 'The allocation of investment and manpower between the various sectors must be based largely on guesswork, and the probability of a balance being achieved is extremely low.' The estimated distribution of investment between the various sectors in the first Five-Year Plan is as follows:

Sector	Investment (Millions £E)	Per cent*
Agriculture	224.2	13.7
Irrigation and Drainage	111.7	6.8
The High Dam	47.3	2.9
Industry	436.2	26.7
Electricity	138.5	8.5
Transport, Communications and Storage	234.2	14.3
Suez Canal	35.0	2.1
Housing	140.0	8.6
Public Establishment	47.6	2.9
Services	101.7	6.2
Changes in Stocks	120.0	7.3
	1,636.4	100.0

*Source: Framework of the General Plan for Economic and Social Development for the Five Years 1960–1 – 1964–5.

As these tables show, the heaviest concentration of investment is in industry and electricity. The industrial sector is expected to generate an increasing share of the national income, and the agricultural sector share to decline. Nevertheless, it is the target for agriculture, which requires a five per cent annual increase in production, which is the most optimistic and the least likely to be attained. The cropped area will only be substantially increased after the completion of the High Dam, i.e. at the end of the second Five-Year Plan, and it is most improbable that productivity from the present area can be increased by five per cent a year. In 1961–2, the second year of the Plan, there was actually a disastrous regression, when about one third of the cotton crop was destroyed by the cotton leafworm. Value added in the agricultural sector fell from £E. 422.1 million in 1960–61 to £E. 372.3 million in 1962.

Nevertheless, despite this severe set-back, the government claims that the estimated overall rate of increase had been achieved in the first four years of the Five-Year Plan. In his report to the National Assembly on 17 November, the Prime Minister, Mr Aly Sabry, said:

Production in the foundation year of the plan, i.e. 1959–60, was estimated at £E. 2,547 million. By the end of the fourth year it reached £E. 3,600 million. This means that 91.6 per cent of the targets for the first Five-Year Plan have been fulfilled by the end of its fourth year.

Since the targets in the agricultural sector had not been reached, those in other sectors must have been exceeded. Mr Sabry declared:

A sum of £E. 929 million has been earmarked for the services sector during the first Five-Year Plan. In four years £E. 993 million was actually spent on this sector, that is, £E. 64 million more than the total allocations for the first five years. It had been decided that the services sector should represent £E. 692 million of the national income, but within the first four years it has become £E. 710 million of the national income. In the field of transport, communication and storage in the first four years, we have reached 111.5 per cent of the target for the first Five-Year Plan; in the public utilities sector, we have reached 98 per cent; and in the field of housing, 98.5 per cent.

Mr Sabry also said: 'The number of workers in the foundation year (1959–60) was about six million. It was decided to increase it to 7,015,000 by the end of the First Development Plan. I take great pleasure in announcing that by the end of the fourth year employment rose to 7,085,000.'

Foreign economic observers have often criticized this rather crude method of illustrating economic progress. By relying on national income and 'value of production' figures, it is possible to conceal wastage, inefficiency and bad planning (although, to be fair, both President Nasser and Mr Sabry have admitted freely in their speeches that these have occurred). There is no means of telling, for instance, whether with a different distribution of investment among the sectors the rate of expansion might not have been much higher. But even through the fog of dubious statistics it is possible to discern something of what has and has not been achieved.

INDUSTRIALIZATION

The rate of physical investment in industry has been high – especially during the past five or six years. Members of the government are apt to exaggerate the lack of industry in Egypt before the Revolution; Egyptian industrialization really began in the 1930s, and between 1938 and 1951 production rose by 138 per cent. But it is true that the heavily protected industrial sector was limited to a very small range of industries. As Dr Aziz Sidqi, Deputy Prime Minister for Industry and Mineral Wealth, told the National Assembly on 12 December 1964: 'In 1952 industries were limited in number and variety – a few spinning mills, some oil-pressing mills, flour mills, cement factories, etc. . . . Today the U.A.R. manufactures almost everything.' He gave as examples of the new products turned out by Egyptian industry since the Revolution: 'Ammonium sulphate, iron and steel products, rubber tyres, medicines, insecticides, dynamite, pencils, ferrous cement, white cement, sanitary installations, opaque glass, cars, lorries, television sets, refrigerators, grain board, cables, tractors, railway wagons, telephone cables, bicycles, water meters, cutlery, electricity meters, electric transformers, gas cylinders, etc.' He added that the products that were already being exported included: 'Tyres, cement, oil products, fertilizers, bicycles, yarn and fabrics and refrigerators.'

Some of the more complex products mentioned by Dr Sidqi are in fact being assembled in Egypt from imported parts rather than manufactured in the country. The buses and cars were designed in Italy (Fiat), the tractors in Yugoslavia, and the television sets in the United States (R.C.A.). But it is also true that each year more of the manufacturing process can be carried out in Egypt so that ultimately they will be wholly Egyptian products, if not designs. Foreign visitors to the Cairo Industrial Exhibition, which was shrewdly timed to coincide with the Second African Summit Conference in July 1964, and to the U.A.R. pavilion at the New York World Fair were surprised at the variety and range of the goods on display. Anyone who has lived in Egypt for the past few years will have noticed the steadily increasing choice of locally produced goods in the shops. Their quality is usually not up to the better foreign equivalents – although even when it is, Egyptians (of both the new and old regime) are inclined to disbelieve it.

But if Egypt is ever to become an industrial power, it has to export manufactured goods as well as make them. Very few Egyptian industries are yet competitive, and since the home market is almost completely protected, it is only the need to export which will make them so. One problem is that the domestic market is expanding so rapidly that in some instances Egypt has become an importer of articles that it used to export a few years ago. Any policy of starving the home market of locally manufactured consumer goods in order to export them has been rejected as inflationary. One possible course, which was being considered in the winter of 1964, was to reduce and standardize the level of consumer credit, which at present is extremely liberal. It is possible, for instance, to buy a refrigerator with a down-payment of only £E. 3 and similar monthly instalments. It is this more than anything which has enabled the new industrial working class to buy consumers' durables, and created and broadened the otherwise very narrow market for them in Egypt. But if Egypt is to export these goods on any large scale, it will have to limit domestic consumption, and the stiffening of instalment credit terms is one way of doing it, unpopular though such action would be.

The government is aware that a drive to increase exports of manufactured goods requires a radical improvement in marketing methods. The great majority of the industries producing these goods are State-owned and, except for textiles, they have mostly been established within the last ten years. Thus they are having to build up their own marketing organization from nothing. In theory they are encouraged to compete with each other in selling abroad, but the results so far have not been very satisfactory. Egyptian industry grew up behind a high protective wall, and the technique of selling in harshly competitive foreign markets is hard to acquire. Egypt's own importing is entirely controlled by the State, which is mainly guided in its choice by the need to be economical with scarce foreign currencies. There is a tendency to expect the same attitude from other countries – that is, to offer their governments a list of Egyptian goods that are available and expect them to choose. The trouble is that the export markets which Egypt particularly wants to penetrate are the industrially developed countries, where importing is in private hands and highly competitive.

At present Egypt has the best chance of increasing its exports of manufactured goods to countries which have a severe foreign exchange problem (including most of the newly independent states in Africa and Asia) and with which it has good political relations. Both these conditions are essential. A country such as Kuwait, for instance, which has all the foreign exchange it needs, is unlikely to import Egyptian manufactures in preference to those of the most technically advanced States, however pro-Egyptian its government. On the other hand, Egypt's trade with Iraq has fluctuated in direct proportion to the temperature of relations between the two countries. The recent sale to Iraq of fifty buses built by the Nasr company in Egypt was as much a demonstration of Iraqi–Egyptian unity as a commercial transaction. There is nothing wrong with this modern example of trade following the flag (which might be compared with imperial preferences) provided that the customer is reasonably satisfied.

Egypt's trade with the African States (except for the Sudan) is still only a tiny proportion of its total trade, and clearly here must lie its biggest challenge and opportunity. For here are countries which, without exception, are short of foreign exchange for their development programmes and are therefore prepared to conclude bilateral barter agreements to obtain manufactured consumer goods. Although Egypt is linked to all these States through the Organization of African Unity, it has the most chance of success where it has the best political relations. It is no accident that Egyptian exports to Algeria rose from £E. 29,000 in 1962 to £E. 875,000 in 1963, the first full year of independence, and to

Tunisia from £E. 84,000 in 1962 to £E. 385,000 in 1963, when President Nasser and President Bourguiba were reconciled after a long period of estrangement.

EMPLOYMENT AND LABOUR

Employment in industry has risen steadily over the past few years. According to the Department of Public Mobilization and Statistics (Statistical Pocket-Book, 1952–63) the number of workers in industry rose from 401,000 in 1952 to 724,000 in 1963. But this eighty per cent increase in eleven years compares with a rise in the value of industrial production during the same period from £E. 313.8 million to £E 952.6 million – which, even translated into real terms by allowing for the depreciation of the Egyptian pound, amounts to considerably more than eighty per cent. As Professor Issawi remarks:

Two general statements may safely be made about the productivity of Egyptian industry: it is rising rather rapidly; and it is still very low compared with that of advanced countries.

The question is whether the government's policies have helped or hindered the increase in productivity which is vital if Egyptian industry is to become competitive. One of the socialist decrees of 1961 fixed the maximum working day in industry at seven hours; the declared object was to increase employment rapidly, and many people predicted that a sharp fall in productivity would result. Dr Sidqi has defended the policy, declaring:

The reduction affected those workers who previously worked as much as twelve hours, ten or nine hours a day. All these are now working for seven hours, but the factories operate either for the same time they did before or more according to the needs of production.

This is done by operating in shifts at many factories, and Dr Sidqi asserted that productivity had actually increased as a result of the measure, 'because productivity of a worker working nine hours is much less in the last two hours of his working day than of the seven hours he is now working'. This is impossible to confirm from the statistics that are available, but it may well be so in view of the Egyptian workers' acceptance of shift-work.

What may have had a more harmful effect on productivity are the various measures that have been taken to protect labour (or 'coddle the workers' as old-fashioned employers would say). Some managers protest despairingly that it is now virtually impossible to sack anyone, however inefficient, lazy, troublesome or unnecessary he may be. Certainly it is true that over the past few years industrial workers have gained the impression that the government is wholly on their side and that they have little to fear whatever they do. A visit to almost any factory or construction site will confirm that a high proportion of the workers are redundant. Apart from almost complete security in their jobs, workers have been given two seats on company boards of directors (out of a maximum of seven) and twenty-five per cent of the profits (ten per cent in cash and fifteen per cent in social security benefits). The share of each worker or employee in the ten per cent that is distributed directly is proportional to his wage or salary, but has a ceiling of £E. 50.

There is, however, another side to this picture. Egyptian society is paternalistic and has been so for many centuries. The country is also overpopulated. Just as in the past the rich man had a host of retainers dependent upon him, so in any office or workshop there are a number of employees whose presence is strictly unnecessary – two men to bring the coffee when only one is needed, two doormen for only one door. It would have been frankly impossible to override this tradition in industry for the sake of streamlined efficiency without a major social upheaval. Paternalism does also have advantages. Egyptian trade-unions do not have the right to strike, and union officials are virtually representatives of the government. So far this system has worked reasonably well; there is no groundswell of industrial discontent, and loss of productivity from 'worker-coddling' has to be set against what might have been lost through go-slow strikes and 'walk-outs'. The trouble is that this situation cannot continue for ever. Whether consciously or unconsciously, Egyptian industrial workers are aware that so far they have benefited most from the country's economic development since the Revolution. In many respects they constitute a privileged class. As one economist close to the government told the author in the winter of 1964:

During the past five years a lot has been done for the workers. Most of the new legislation has been in their favour. Now we have to reduce the costs of production in order to make our industries more competitive, which means that there can be no new benefits for the workers for the time being.

In other words there is to be a wage freeze in Egyptian industry, although since other privileges and benefits are probably more important than actual cash wages it would be more correct to call it a 'status freeze'. The workers did not have to struggle for their gains; they were decreed by the government. The freeze will similarly be imposed from above, but it would seem contrary to human nature that the workers should accept this without murmur. Although the government has great authority, and there is some understanding and acceptance among the public of the need for belt-tightening at Egypt's present stage of development, some industrial discontent may be expected in the coming years.

DISTRIBUTION OF INCOME

Again the lack of statistics makes impossible any precise estimate of the distribution of income in present-day Egypt and of the extent to which it has changed since the Revolution. But some indications can be derived from simple observation of Egyptian society and changes in the pattern of consumption. Land reform, nationalizations and sequestrations have reduced the gap between rich and poor. The multi-millionaire pashas who, like their monarch, thought nothing of gambling away a few thousand pounds every night in a Riviera casino do not exist in Egypt today; their palaces and villas are closed or have been turned into flats or hotels. Even for several years after the Revolution there was still some conspicuous consumption of the kind for which the *ancien régime* was famous – such as dinner parties for forty with a 'suffragi' behind each chair. But since the socialist decrees of 1961 this has disappeared. On the other hand, the declared aim of these decrees – that no one in Egypt should have an income of more than £E. 5,000 a year – has clearly not been achieved. There are still some families who own agricultural land, buildings, furniture, jewels, and shares worth considerably more than £E. 1 million, although the lack of outlets for private investment ensures that their incomes are not proportionately high. For obvious reasons they do not spend lavishly.

The reduction in spending by the very rich has affected the large class of servants, chauffeurs, gardeners, messengers and watchmen who worked for them. For every rich man in pre-revolutionary Egypt, there were scores who picked up the crumbs that fell from his table. Some of these have found work in the new hotels or the many foreign embassies that have opened in Cairo since the Revolution (the large foreign communities of Greeks, Italians and Levantines, now no longer in Egypt, have to some extent been replaced by a new type of more transitory foreigner – U.N.-employees, experts, engineers, etc.). Nevertheless, it is quite common to find old retainers remaining with their employers unpaid because they have nowhere else to go – like liberated slaves, whom they resemble in many ways.

Industrialization, increased industrial wages, and distribution of profits, combined with various measures to hold down the cost of living, have substantially increased the incomes of the urban working class. According to the Prime Minister, Mr Sabry: 'At the time of the Revolution, wages were estimated at £E. 349 million, in 1959–60 they reached £E. 549.5 million, and at the end of the fourth year of the Plan they were £E. 770.3 million.' The official wholesale price index showed a sharp increase from 343 in 1952 (1939 = 100) to 415 in 1956, but from then onwards held steady between 415 and 425. These figures certainly underestimate the amount of inflation because they are based on officially controlled prices which are frequently evaded. The cost of living has been rising steadily a few per cent each year for the past few years. However, the inflation has been trotting rather than galloping, and there is no doubt whatever that the mass of city-dwellers have enjoyed a substantial increase in real as well as in money income.

As is to be expected among people living at such a very low income level, most of this extra income has been spent on food. Mr Sabry himself told the National Assembly:

In 1952 we imported only 4,600 tons of meat. In 1959–60 local production amounted to 157,000 tons, and we imported 15,100 tons of livestock, meat and poultry. In 1964 local production was 189,000 tons, and imports amounted to 52,500 tons. With regard to flour, 1952 imports amounted to 144,000 tons. We imported 442,000 tons in the 1959–60 fiscal year and 693,000 tons in the 1963–4 fiscal year. In 1952 we did not import wheat, and consumption amounted to one million tons a year. This year's consumption amounted to 2,315,000 tons.

Consumption of basic foodstuffs in Egypt, such as wheat, maize, sugar, rice and tea, has been rising at the rate of between five and ten per cent a year (compared with an annual population increase of 2.5–2.8 per cent). Since the greater part of this increased consumption has been in the cities and towns, the urban working class is eating very much more than it did before. (This is borne out by the remarkable number of cheap café-restaurants selling rice, *foul*, *falafil*, etc., which have opened in Cairo in recent years.) In 1964–5 food imports will cost £E. 140 million. The government expects this extraordinary increase to continue and estimates that by 1970 consumption of wheat and flour will have risen to 4,700,000 tons; maize to 2,800,000 tons; and meat and fish to 464,000 tons.

The increased consumption would have been much less if the government had allowed the cost of living to rise more than it has. Price controls; reductions in house rents, bus and train fares; and food subsidies, which in 1964–5 will amount to more than £E. 55 million, have been introduced to prevent this. The chain of government retail cooperative shops has contributed much towards providing the public with meat, vegetables and groceries at reasonable prices. For this reason the cooperatives are generally popular with the public (and intensely unpopular with the private retailers) despite the long queues which are normal because supplies are limited, the frequent rudeness and inefficiency of the employees, and recently the discovery that some of them were holding back goods to sell them at a profit to the independent butchers and grocers. The government has regularly reaffirmed its policy of holding down prices by these measures although they have greatly added to its economic difficulties. In November 1964 it went further and announced that prices of essentials would be restored to their 1961 level. (A cartoon in *al-Ahram* showed two women at the end of an immense queue in front of a cooperative. One is saying to the other: 'Lucky we are at the end, because by the time we get to the front prices will have gone down.')

Liberal economists regard these 'distortions of the market' with extreme disapproval, failing to acknowledge the great humanitarian benefits that they have brought to the Egyptian urban working class. Such 'distortions' are an essential part of Nasser's doctrine that the mass of the people (workers and *fellahin*) have been deprived for so long that they deserve to be compensated. The most cogent criticism that can be made of them is that they have benefited the workers very much more than the *fellahin*, and the 'status freeze' for the workers which the government now proposes is essentially an effort to direct some of the prosperity of the towns to the countryside. The only simple way to do this is to make the townspeople pay more for home-produced food, and an indication that the government has this in mind was the decision in November 1964 to remove all price controls from home-produced, but not from imported meat, so as to encourage the *fellahin* to rear more livestock.

Foreign residents in Egypt tend to resent the U.N. statistical estimate (proudly reproduced by the government to attract tourists) that Cairo is the cheapest major capital in the world. They say that they spend as much in a month as they would in Athens, Ankara or even Beirut. The explanation is that Cairo is still very cheap for those who can subsist on Egyptian-made goods and live as far as possible in an Egyptian style (that is, eating typical Egyptian food and wearing Egyptian-made clothing). Anything imported (such as Scotch whisky at £E. 4.5 to £E. 5 a bottle) or bought on the black market is very expensive. In the winter of 1964, for example, batteries for ubiquitous transistor radios were unobtainable except on the black market at £E. 0.15 each (about 2s. 6d.). Consumers' durable goods such as refrigerators (8 cu.ft for £E. 100) or gas heaters (£E. 35) which are produced by 100 per cent protected Egyptian industries are also expensive. Against this must be set the fact that wages are still low in Egypt (and there is a high rate of under-employment) so that anything which involves in its production a high proportion of unskilled labour is normally cheap. Foreign residents now pay their servants between £E. 12 and £E. 20 a month, but Egyptians pay half this or less. Egypt, in other words, is in that condition common to countries which are halfway between being under-developed and developed; it is both cheap and expensive at the same time, and the cost of living is much higher for the rich than for the poor.

Wages and salaries are both low, but for the fully employed wages compare favourably with salaries. In industry the minimum wage of £E. 0.25 for anyone over eighteen years of age has been generally observed, and most workers in state-owned factories earn more than this for their statutory seven-hour day, forty-two-hour week. At the Iron and Steel Factory at Helwan, for instance, unskilled workers receive between £E. 30 and £E. 35 a month , and skilled workers from £E. 60 to £E. 70. And this is apart from substantial fringe benefits such as free medical attention at the factory clinic and low-rent housing provided by the company. At the Spinning and Weaving Factory in Mehalla el-Kubra a midday meal is provided for all the 21,000 workers at seven piastres (about 1s. 2d.) to which the company contributes half the cost.

A young university graduate, on the other hand, who is fortunate enough to find immediate employment on leaving the university, may expect a salary of £E. 20 to £E. 25 a month for several years, even if he is a well-qualified doctor or engineer. In the civil service the highest grade (Under-Secretary of State) earns £E. 3,000 a year. In industry a board chairman gets £E. 4,000 a year 'compared with the £E. 30,000 formerly paid to each member of the board in some cases'. (Dr Aziz Sidqi, Speech to National Assembly, 12 December 1964.)

Some critics believe that Egypt has gone too far in its policy of reducing discrepancies, and that current salary ranges are not wide enough to provide incentives. They point out that the range is considerably wider in the Soviet Union. However, the official salary scale does not give the whole picture. During 1964 the Cairo Press revealed that a substantial number of people in the higher ranks of industry and the civil service were receiving travel and other allowances which in some cases came to more than their basic salaries. Others were holding three or four jobs and drawing salaries from each. The Ministry of Finance determined that in future total allowances should never amount to more than thirty per cent of the basic salary; but because of the difficulty of forcing senior government servants to accept such a sharp cut in income, many of the basic salaries had to be raised substantially in compensation.

MANAGEMENT, ORGANIZATION AND BUREAUCRACY

Whether or not the lack of incentive in wage and salary scales is a contributing factor, Egypt is short both of skilled top-level managers and of trained foremen in the intermediate range. The problem is made worse by the overstaffing which we have already mentioned and an ancient tradition of bureaucracy which dies very hard. Where good managers have been found the results have been remarkable, and the Egyptian contractors Othman Ahmed Othman, who have carried out seventy per cent of the work on the High Dam, the Egyptian Petroleum Organization and the Suez Canal Authority all have encouraging records. Some of the best managers have been young officer-engineers from the Egyptian army selected for their ability rather than their rank or connexions.

In a series of penetrating articles on 'Administration and the Problem of Bureaucracy', the editor-in-chief of al-Ahram, Muhammad Hasanein Heykal, pointed out that after the Revolution the government was well aware of the shortcomings in the old bureaucratic system but could not dispense with it. At first it had to run the country through men who held to the old ways and methods, because it had no one else to put in their place. But as the Revolution advanced, the State tried to limit the 'bureaucratic danger' by surrounding the old guard with a new one, of which the Suez Canal Authority and the Agrarian Reform and Desert Reclamation Authority are examples. This new guard has acted as a 'spearhead of the national effort', but inevitably it has incurred the severe hostility of the old one. Heykal concludes that the ultimate responsibility does not lie with the bureaucrats themselves, but with the political system which controls them. Bureaucrats cannot be expected to change their mentality merely because the State has changed its political colour.

In this Mr Heykal is almost certainly correct. The government has done something to improve the situation by establishing Institutes of Vocational Training and Personnel Management, as well as a Vocational Training and Productivity Centre, with the aid of the United Nations and the International Labour Organization; but a really effective reform requires a complete change in the atmosphere of government departments. Anyone who has had to deal with the older established government ministries and enterprises will have discovered the extreme timidity and reluctance to take responsibility of all employees except the very highest. This is partly, although not entirely, the result of overstaffing. Because there is usually not enough work for all the employees, new and unnecessary regulations have to be created to occupy them. Red tape grows longer and the employees, who know instinctively that their job is really unnecessary, lose any independence of judgement that they may have had when they started. This is something that clearly cannot be changed overnight, for it is the consequence of overpopulation and underemployment. But it is also a fact that the extreme authoritarianism of Egyptian society and government does much to discourage initiative and enterprise. In cases of emergency, where something has gone radically wrong – as in 1964, when the Cairo municipal bus services had hundreds of buses idle through a lack of spare parts, or the crisis at Alexandria Port, where millions of pounds worth of essential goods were rotting on the wharves because they had not received customs clearances – drastic action is taken to put things right; but it is taken from the top by someone with special power to cut through the red tape. The system is not permanently reformed.

The whole question of bureaucracy has become more important with the nationalizations of the last five years. In one way or another, the government machine now controls most of the country's economic life, and though the government itself is aware of the dangers that this represents, it does not yet have a clear idea of what to do about it. During 1964 there were frequent rumours that State-owned companies or groups of companies (formed by the amalgamation of nationalized or semi-nationalized firms) would be made autonomous and encouraged to compete with each other. The issue of how far the profit motive should have a place in Egyptian socialism was discussed at length in the Press, but by the end of the year the government had given no clear lead in the matter.

The dominating view was that the dangers of bureaucracy and the need to associate the people more closely with the State machine could best be dealt with through the Arab Socialist Union, and in December 1964 the government administration was reorganized with the object of giving the A.S.U. some control over government departments. It will need time to see whether this reform is effective.

Another development in late 1964 was the transformation of the Civil Service Department into a Central Agency for Organization and Administration with higher status and wider powers. This has yet to prove its effectiveness, but it could be very beneficial.

CURRENCY AND BALANCE OF PAYMENTS

During the First World War the direct ties between Egypt's currency and gold were severed, and the Egyptian pound became linked to sterling. In 1947 Egypt left the sterling area, in 1948 the agreement for the automatic conversion of sterling into Egyptian pounds was ended, and Egypt's sterling balances, which stood as high as £E. 405 million in 1945, were blocked. A series of agreements over the following years enabled Egypt to draw on these balances, and it used these partly to build up its gold cover to the note issue. By the end of 1960 this gold reserve stood at £E. 60.6 million and it remained stable until some £E. 15 million were sold on the Swiss markets in January 1965 to repay some short-term credits from Western banks which had been delayed.

Since 1949 there has been no official devaluation of the Egyptian pound, but through a system of premia and discounts a *de facto* devaluation in relation to the main convertible currencies was achieved. In December 1961 the situation was regularized with a twenty per cent surcharge for import payments and a twenty per cent premium for exports, applied equally to trade with all countries, and in May 1962 a uniform premium of twenty-five per cent was applied to all bank transfers in settlement of exports and payment of services. Since December 1961 the import or export of Egyptian bank-notes has been prohibited, which means that their value on free exchange markets outside Egypt is no longer any indication of the health of the Egyptian economy.

Egypt now has a currency system which is fully controlled by the State, with all the normal advantages and disadvantages that this implies. On the one hand the Egyptian economy is insulated from external factors (such as the devaluation of sterling), and the Egyptian pound is not tied to the balance of payments. Under the pre-1948 system a deficit in the balance of payments would have automatically imposed deflation, which would effectively have disposed of Egypt's Five-Year Plans. On the other hand, there is the extreme inconvenience in a number of ways of having a currency with no international value, and there is no restraining power on the government's control of the economy.

It is certainly arguable that such a system is imperative for Egypt during its present stage of development, but the trouble is that once it is established it is extremely difficult to relax. Furthermore, like prohibition, rigid currency control makes every citizen (and every tourist) a potential criminal because of the ease and attraction of smuggling.

Once Egypt had been set on a course of breakneck development, it was inevitable that the country should suffer severe balance of payments difficulties. Free foreign exchange reserves have hovered around the $6 million mark since 1962 and the government lives from hand-to-mouth, making day-by-day decisions to allocate foreign currencies where they are most needed. The Deputy Prime Minister for Finance, Dr Kaissouny, has gone so far as to say that no developing country ought to have any substantial foreign currency reserves, because this would merely mean that resources which should be employed were lying idle. This is all very well provided that the government is realistic in its forecasts of the country's balance of payments position, but the Egyptian government has been consistently over-optimistic. The most striking example was the key estimate in the first Five-Year Plan that imports would actually decline from £E. 229.2 million in 1959–60 to £E. 214.9 million in 1964–5, whereas the entire character of the Plan made it inevitable that imports, especially of capital goods, would rise steeply. In fact they rose to £E. 238.5 million in 1961, £E. 301 million in 1962, and to the astonishing figure of £E. 398 million in 1964 (only partly inflated by the *de facto* devaluation), despite the most severe restrictions on the importing of consumer goods.

The result was that instead of improving, the balance of payments situation worsened. In the summer of 1964 a number of factories were working below capacity because of the lack of foreign exchange, which had delayed the import of essential raw materials or machine spare parts.

Egypt's Foreign Trade (£E. million)*

	Imports	Exports
1910	23.6	28.9
1920	104.2	92.0
1930	47.5	32.9
1940	32.4	30.0
1950	216.8	175.4
1955	187.2	146.0
1956	186.1	142.3
1957	182.6	171.6
1958	240.1	166.3
1959	222.1	160.5
1960	232.5	197.8
1961	238.5	161.2
1962	301.0	158.3
1963	398.4	226.8

*Source: Dept of Public Mobilization and Statistics.

The situation would have been very much worse still but for three factors. One was the recovery of cotton production after the disastrous 1961–2 season and the improved prices paid for Egyptian long staples in 1963 and 1964 (partly due to two successive failures in the Sudanese cotton harvest); another was the steady increase in Suez Canal tolls; and the third was the tourist revenue.

Suez Canal tolls have risen as more and bigger ships have used it.

	(£E. million)*
1955	31.8
1956	29.3
1957	24.3
1958	43.0
1959	44.4
1960	50.1
1961	51.2
1962	53.7
1963	71.1
1964	77.0

*Sources: Central Bank of Egypt Research Department and Suez Canal Authority.

The sudden increase between 1962 and 1963 is partly due to the change, as of 31 December 1962, from converting Canal receipts at the old official rate of £E. 1 = $2.87 to the new (and more realistic) rate of £E. 1 = $2.30; but further sharp increases can be expected as a result of ambitious plans to widen and deepen the Canal so that the largest tankers can pass through it. The efficiency and enterprise with which the Suez Canal Authority has been run by a young officer engineer, Mahmoud Yunes, who has consistently followed a policy of investing heavily in the improvement of the Canal to raise revenues, has been one of the outstanding achievements of the regime.

Tourism is already an important source of income for Egypt, and the potential expansion is enormous. Egypt not only has antiquities which schoolboys everywhere have heard of, but two fine and largely undeveloped coastlines, together with a climate which is superb during the spring and autumn in Lower Egypt and in Upper Egypt during the winter. It is only really oppressive in August, and even this is not enough to deter many present-day tourists – especially Americans and Scandinavians.

Dr Hatem, the Deputy Prime Minister for Culture and National Guidance, who has been in charge of the tourist drive, is undoubtedly right in believing that tourist income could be raised from its present level of about £E. 25 million to £E. 100 million in a few years, and although his heavy hotel-building programme ('a new hotel opened every month') has been expensive, its potential return in foreign currency income is greater than that of any other industry. But here, as elsewhere in the economy, an easy over-optimism and lack of planning have led to serious mistakes. In 1963–4 tourists were encouraged to come to Egypt when there were not enough completed hotels to receive them or trained staff to look after them. The 'Save Abu Simbel' campaign gave Egypt invaluable publicity throughout the world; but elderly matrons from Missouri who arrived at their hotel in Upper Egypt to find that the rooms they had booked were already occupied by elderly matrons from Ohio and that they would have to pass the night on chairs in the lounge were not mollified to be told by an Egyptian official that this was 'proof of the success of the tourist drive'. In 1964–5, there were signs that the season was not as good as the previous year; even more serious, although the number of tourists coming to Egypt in 1963 was thirty-nine per cent higher than in 1962, the total number of 'tourist nights' only rose by 1.3 per cent. The new tourists being attracted to Egypt were mostly middle-class and lower-middle-class Europeans and Americans who had a few days to spend before going on to Beirut or Athens. They paid for their inclusive tours in advance and brought little cash with them. This trend is probably inevitable, because the real expansion in the tourist market is among such people rather than the leisured rich of the kind who used to spend three months wintering in Egypt sixty years ago. But this does not seem to have been borne in mind when some of the new hotels in Egypt were planned.

FOREIGN INVESTMENTS

The gravest consequence of Egypt's chronic balance of payments difficulties is that the country has acquired a bad reputation for the payment of commercial debts. In 1963 it was still true to say that Egypt enjoyed a good reputation overall, because if payments were delayed they were always made in the end. But the delays were becoming longer, until some creditors became exasperated. One small but significant example was that many foreign booksellers stopped shipments to Egypt in 1964 because payments were two or three years behind. In July 1964 the Sudanese–Egyptian payments agreement was cancelled, and Sudanese exports to Egypt of camels and meat ceased because Egypt had failed to pay for them. Meanwhile Egypt's liabilities from interest charges and repayment of principal were piling up at an alarming rate. Payment of compensation to the Suez Canal Company of £E. 28.3 million had actually been completed one year earlier than agreed in the 1958 settlement, but there remained compensation for British, French, Belgian, Swiss, Lebanese and other nationalized and sequestrated property. As we have seen, it was persistent delay in making these payments which caused the I.B.R.D. to announce that it was making no more loans to Egypt.

The following foreign loans and credit facilities (excluding military credits) have been made available to Egypt since December 1957:

		(£E. million)
From Communist states		
U.S.S.R.		332.5
Czechoslovakia		62.0
East Germany		45.0
Poland		24.4
Hungary		12.0
Yugoslavia		7.0
	Total:	482.9
From non-Communist states		
U.S.A.		535.6
West Germany		93.0
Italy		92.9
Japan		17.0
France		10.0
Britain		5.4
Netherlands		5.0

From non-Communist states (*continued*)	(£E. million)
Switzerland	4.0
Sweden	3.3
Others	6.3
Total:	782.5
I.B.R.D.	19.7
International Monetary Fund	36.0
Grand Total:	1,321.1

These figures are, however, only estimates. No complete list of foreign aid to Egypt is available from official sources, and this one has been compiled by adding to the most recent official figures (1961) such as have since been announced in the Press and elsewhere. It is reasonably accurate, but does not give the breakdown of long-term and short-term loans – although it may be assumed that almost all the loans from Communist sources are long-term.

The greater part of American aid since 1959 has been in the form of U.S. counterpart funds related to PL 480 (that is surplus wheat, meat, chicken, etc.), and these are repayable in Egyptian currency – most of which is then re-lent to Egypt for development with interest at four per cent and repayment in thirty years. Apart from this, most of the loans from Western sources take the form of short-term credits through the banks. Egypt has generally shown a preference for buying its capital goods, wherever possible, from the Western countries rather than the Communist bloc, and this is why such a high proportion of loans and credits from the latter has not been used. By the end of 1964 however, it was clear to the government that this policy was adding to Egypt's difficulties and that more Eastern credits would have to be used.

In early 1964 Egypt received a long-term loan of £E. 25 million from the Kuwait Government and a further £E. 10 million from the Kuwaiti Arab Development Fund for the improvement of the Suez Canal. Such help provided important relief during a crucial period, but by the end of the year it was reported that Egypt was already seeking a further loan from

Kuwait. One possibility that was being explored was that Egypt should make some of its repayments in the form of manufactured goods, such as underwear, pyjamas or shoes, to those creditor countries like the Soviet Union and the Sudan which might prefer to have them immediately rather than wait an interminable period for repayment in convertible currency.

SAVINGS, TAXATION AND WASTE

Despite the growth of deposit banking, post-office savings and insurance since the First World War, the rate of saving in Egypt is still very low. The Prime Minister told the National Assembly on 17 November 1964: 'Savings in our society constitute not more than five per cent of national income, whereas the average rate of savings in all advanced countries is not less than twenty per cent.'

The reason for this is not, as it used to be, that Egyptians are unfamiliar with cheques and banks and prefer to hoard their money at home. A visit to any bank in Egypt shows that the banking habit has spread throughout society. Nationalization and sequestrations and the power of the Taxation Department to seize bank deposits have caused some of the wealthier classes to prefer holding their money in buildings, furniture, jewellery or *objets d'art*, but the chief reason for the low rate of saving is that the increase in the national income is all being consumed. The government's estimate is that the national income rose by 19.2 per cent in the first three years of the first Five-Year Plan and consumption by nineteen per cent. The greater part of this increase was in food consumption, and this is the normal consequence of redistributing income in favour of the working class. However, the urgent need to increase savings has made the government consider various ways of encouraging the habit among the public. It was decided in late 1964 to raise the rate of interest on post-office savings from three to 3.5 per cent and to launch a savings drive.

Since the socialist decrees of 1961, Egypt has had one of the most steeply progressive rates of taxation in the world. Income tax rises from twenty-five per cent on the £E. 1,000–1,500 group to ninety per cent on incomes over £E. 10,000. Since 1939 there have been four categories of income tax: on dividends and interest; on profits of financial, commercial and industrial enterprises; on incomes of the liberal professions; and on wages and salaries. With an exemption limit on wages of £E. 0.50 per day, a high proportion of industrial workers, employees and government servants should now be paying income tax; but the Department of Taxation has still substantially to improve the methods of collection, for evasion is widespread.

Apart from income tax, there is a land tax assessed on the rental value of agricultural land and a tax on built property. But providing by far the most important source of revenue are the indirect taxes of customs and excise duties. Although export duties have been reduced or abolished, customs duties on capital goods have been reduced, and imports of all manufactured consumer goods have either declined or ceased altogether, this has been more than offset by increased duties on and consumption of coffee, tea, tobacco and alcoholic drinks.

How far are waste and corruption a serious problem in present-day Egypt? The question is crucial, because it was these more than anything else that caused the young Egyptian nationalist's disgust with the monarch. There can be no doubt whatever that at the highest level – among Vice-Presidents, Ministers, and permanent heads of government departments – the standard of economic morality is very much higher than it was before the Revolution. President Nasser himself has dealt ruthlessly with any senior government official touched by financial scandal, and although some of his bitter enemies have tried to suggest from time to time that he or one of his Ministers is living a life of secret luxury or salting away funds in Geneva, no one seriously believes it. The net gain to the country of the public's confidence that ten per cent of every foreign loan is not going into the private pockets of government officials is immense.

Below the higher offices of the State, however, the situation has changed very little since before the Revolution. The granting of special favours in return for *baksheesh* is still a widespread practice in the police, customs and other government services.

It is difficult to stamp out such a hallowed tradition, especially while salaries remain low and government officials are so strongly tempted to use their position to supplement their incomes. Moreover the immense expansion of State power has increased the opportunities for corruption. Stringent import controls, for instance, have increased the potential value of import licences, and in 1964 a serious case of bribery by businessmen of Import Department officials came to light. We have already mentioned the widespread corruption among government retail cooperatives and the effect of strict currency control in making smuggling a common practice. The thousands of residents of Egypt, both Egyptian and foreign, who still have fortunes inside the country that they wish for one reason or another to take out, will in the main not shrink from using any kind of illegal means to export their capital.

The severe restrictions on foreign travel (which are essentially a form of currency control) have enormously increased the attraction of employment likely to take anyone out of the country. The inability to travel is a severe hardship for the Egyptian upper middle classes today, and several university students from what used to be called 'good families' have told the author that they aim to join the diplomatic service for this reason alone. There is a distinct danger, indeed, that a new class will emerge in Egypt with privileges derived from office rather than property or land. The government showed some awareness of this in November 1964 when it decided, as part of its economy measures, to close down many of its representative offices abroad (commercial, tourist, etc.) which had been duplicating the work of embassies, and at home to sell government cars to the employees using them. It was revealed that the running of these cars cost the government more than £E. 1 million a year, while it had very little power to ensure that they were not being misused.

Corruption and waste are two aspects of the same problem, which is one of the most serious that the Egyptian Government has to face. Nothing would do more to undermine the Revolution than a return to the cynical self-indulgence of the governing class which was so characteristic of the Farouk era.

10 The Land and the *Fellah*

Here man belongs to the land; it is not the land that belongs to him. (Father Henry Ayrout.)

'Know-how' is not one of the things that its [Egypt's] agriculture lacks, nor was ignorance of agricultural techniques a cause of peasant poverty. On the contrary, the *fellahin* are excellent farmers, skilled and hard-working. In these respects Egypt was not an under-developed country; it was not the land which was neglected, but its cultivators. (Doreen Warriner.)

Very few have failed to be charmed by the valley and Delta of the Lower Nile – the serene palm trees, the brilliant green clover standing against the chocolate earth and a soft blue sky, the somnolent buffaloes cooling themselves in the canals, and the overwhelming impression of ancient fertile land carefully and lovingly tended. But the civilized beauty of the Egyptian country-side should not conceal the fact that most of the people who inhabit it are as poor, hungry and diseased as anywhere on earth.

About seventy per cent of the Egyptian people are *fellahin*, but it cannot be said that the remaining thirty per cent have cared much about peasant poverty. 'They have always lived like that, so they expect nothing different' is a typical comment of an Egyptian town-dweller. The present regime, many of whose leaders, like President Nasser himself, are the sons or grandsons of *fellahin*, are aware that the miserable condition of Egypt's peasantry is the chief cause of the country's under-development. But the problem grows more serious as the heavy emphasis on industrialization widens still further the gap between town and country.

Egyptian agriculture is highly distinctive for several reasons. The land is the most productive in the world, but it is extremely limited in area (about six million acres, or three per cent of the country's total), and since the rainfall in Egypt is negligible except near the north coast, it is all irrigated. For these reasons it is expensive, highly profitable and overcrowded, and because it is irrigated rather than rain-fed, the rights of individual ownership have always been limited by the powers of the pharaoh, khedive, government or whoever has controlled the source of irrigation, the River Nile.

Under the Pharaohs, the Arabs and the Mamelukes, privileged groups, notably the priests and military chieftains, secured some *de facto* rights of property over the land, even to the point of transferring ownership through gifts or inheritance, but the central power of the State was always able to recover its rights in time. Land ownership in Egypt remained essentially different both from the system in Western Europe and in other countries conquered by Islam.

In the early seventeenth century the Ottomans devised the idea of the *iltizam* ('obligation' in Arabic) as a means of raising money. The *multazamin* were required to raise a certain sum in taxes from the district allocated to them, and in the periods when the central power was weak they acquired something of the status of feudal barons. In his struggle with the Mamelukes, Napoleon tried to establish private property rights for the *fellahin*, but the French occupation was too short for the system to take root. A few years later, Muhammad Aly destroyed the Mamelukes and re-established a strong centralized government; he then abolished the *iltizam* and established a cadastre for all Egypt's cultivated land, which at that time amounted to two million acres. Part of this land he granted to the *fellahin* in usufruct and in small plots of three to five acres, but he also leased vast estates to members of his family, military chiefs and high State officials from the Turco-Egyptian ruling class. He retained ownership of the land, but the profits of farming now belonged to the cultivators. From towards the end of his reign until the end of the nineteenth century, the rights of private property were steadily extended.

Muhammad Aly intentionally laid the foundations of a hereditary landed aristocracy which grew steadily in power and wealth throughout the century, and it is easy to see that the great mass of the *fellahin* were incapable of preventing this from happening at their expense. The total amount of cultivable land was small, and individual farms were continually being divided through inheritance. After Muhammad Aly's death in 1849, Egyptian industries collapsed, so there was no alternative employment to absorb the surplus population on the land. As successive khedives required more money, it was the *fellahin*, not the new landed aristocracy, that were forced to provide it.

After the deposition of the super-extravagant Khedive Ismail and the British occupation, the lot of the *fellahin* improved for a time. The corvée was abolished and replaced by paid labour; taxes were reduced through financial retrenchment; and the area of land under permanent irrigation was greatly extended through hydraulic improvements on the river and canals. The last two decades of the nineteenth century were probably the most prosperous that the Egyptian countryside has seen before or since.

For a brief period production outpaced the increase in population, but this did not last. Between 1897 and 1947 the cultivated area increased by fourteen per cent and the cropped area by thirty-seven per cent, but the population doubled. Yields per acre also increased fairly steadily, and although there are no precise figures for agricultural production during this period, it is thought that it kept either just ahead of or just behind the increase in population.

In 1947 the *per capita* real income of Egypt's rural population was just about what it had been fifty years before, but the distribution of income had become still more uneven. The increasing population pressure combined with the relatively small increase in the cultivated area steadily to swell the number of small farmers owning less than five *feddans*.

Year	Small holdings (Below 5 *feddans*)		Medium holdings (5–50 *feddans*)		Large holdings (above 50 *feddans*)	
	landowners	land	landowners	land	landowners	land
1894	83.3	21.7	15.4	34.3	1.3	44
1914	91.3	26.7	8.5	30.4	0.8	43.9
1930	93.1	31.6	6.3	29.7	0.6	38.7
1952	94.3	35.4	5.2	30.4	0.5	34.2

The situation was far worse even than this table suggests, however. Two *feddans* of land constitute an absolute minimum from which a *fellahin* family can make a living, and in 1952 there were 2,018,100 who owned less than one *feddan*. They were seventy-two per cent of all proprietors, and they owned only thirteen per cent of cultivable land. In addition there were about 1.5 million families (about eight million people) who owned no land at all and lived by share-cropping or casual labour. At the other end of the scale 280 proprietors owned 583,400 *feddans* (of which 178,000 *feddans* were the property of the royal family).

As it became increasingly difficult for the *fellahin* to make a living for their families from their dwindling plots of land, more and more *fellahin* were forced either to try renting or share-cropping on an additional small area, or lease out their own plot and try to find employment as labourers. In either case the trend was the same. Between 1939 and 1949 the proportion of land that was rented rose from seventeen to sixty per cent. The common impression that the typical Egyptian *fellah* was a peasant owner-cultivator had become wholly false. At the same time the demand for land had forced up the price from about £E. 200 a *feddan* before the Second World War to about £E. 800 just before the Revolution. Rents more than quadrupled, and conditions were becoming more and more unfavourable to the tenant. Moreover, rents rose more than net output, so that it became more advantageous for the landowner to lease his land than to farm it himself. Rents varied fairly widely between different estates and between different parts of the Delta and Valley, but in 1952 the average rent level for the whole country was about £E. 30 an acre, equivalent to some fifty per cent of the gross produce. An absentee owner of a 5,000-acre estate could accordingly count on a gross income of £E. 150,000, while the gross value of their produce for the vast majority who owned two *feddans* or less was under £E. 120. Net income per head of the active agricultural population in Egypt was estimated at £E. 34 in 1953, compared with an average net income for the active agricultural population in Western Europe of £E. 190.

Nasser's Egypt

As Doreen Warriner remarks:

The status of the small tenant-cultivator on a holding of two or three acres was that of a labourer rather than of a tenant. Formerly (i.e. before land reform) he had no security of tenure and no incentive and no means to invest, since the landowner undertook this function, and his income barely covered his needs. His position was better than that of the casual labourer only in so far as he was more regularly employed.

Moreover, he had almost no chance of ever improving his position, however hard or skilfully he worked his land.

The high price of land made it impossible for the small tenant-cultivator to purchase land. High rents and debts prevented him from accumulating the necessary capital. In 1947 a farmer would have needed to save £E. 2,350 to purchase five acres of land, together with the necessary capital equipment. For labourers with an agricultural wage of 9.4 piastres per day (about 1s. 10d.) the purchase of land at this price is clearly out of the question.

Because of his poverty and the cheapness of labour, the 'typical' *fellah* (or one owning less than five *feddans*) has neither the ability nor incentive to use modern techniques. Most of the simple tools he uses are depicted on the walls of the Pharaohs' tombs. He scratches the soil with a primitive plough pulled by a buffalo or calf, clears the weeds with a short-handled hoe, harvests corn and rice with a sickle, threshes them by piling them up and driving a heavy wooden sledge over them, and winnows them in the wind. For irrigation, which is the main part of his work, he raises the water with *sakias* – wooden water-wheels pulled by an ox – or more probably (since the *sakia* is expensive) by hand with the Archimedes screw or *shadoof* – a horizontal bar on a forked stick with a weight at one end and a bucket on the other. The vital and delicate task of levelling the land to receive the water he does by hand and eye.

For cotton the work is rather different, and child labour is widely used. Children are the right height for harvesting the cotton and for the important work of searching the backs of leaves for the cotton worm. They are paid less than a shilling for an eight- or ten-hour day. Motor pumps for drainage and irrigation and tractors are only in general use on the medium and large estates and on the State farms.

Since Muhammad Aly began replacing basin with perennial irrigation, work on the land has been intensified. Previously, the *fellahin* sowed in the autumn on the mud left by the Nile flood and harvested in the early summer. For the rest of the year the land lay fallow waiting for the next flood. Now most of the land is perennially irrigated (and 700,000 more *feddans* in Upper Egypt will be converted from basin to perennial when the High Dam is finished).

With perennial irrigation the *fellah* has more work to do, but because of the rural overpopulation, there is still much unemployment and underemployment. As Jean and Simone Lacouture shrewdly observe in *Egypt in Transition*:

The country districts have such a surplus of labour that half the population can spend its time napping, without affecting the bustling appearance of the fields. That is why the most hard-working people can give the impression of being the idlest.

Egyptian country life is a curious mixture of drudgery and unemployment, both equally demoralizing.

When there is work to be done, it is long drawn out and back-breaking. For much of the year the *fellah* suffers burning heat, but because of the perpetual dampness of the soil and mud in which he works, he is bitterly cold during the short Egyptian winter. He is also undernourished and in poor health. We have already mentioned some of the common endemic diseases of the Egyptian countryside. Although naturally of good physique, the *fellah* never fully enjoys good health after adolescence. Because there is still less perennial irrigation in Upper Egypt than in the Delta, the Upper Egyptians suffer less from the parasitic water-borne diseases than the northerners and are preferred for employment in heavy labouring work. For the same reason the women, who rarely work in the fields except as cotton pickers, enjoy better health than the men.

Eighty per cent of the *fellah*'s calories come from maize bread, of which he eats up to three pounds a day. The rest of his diet consists of onions, turnip, peppers or cucumber, which he eats raw, or beans, marrows, lentils and rice which are cooked for the evening meal on a primus stove or one fuelled with dry cotton branches or maize leaves. At some seasons he will have goat's cheese, dates, melon, or a piece of sugar-cane to suck; on very rare occasions, he eats meat.

Over ninety per cent of the village houses are made of mud brick dried in the sun. The rafters are strong enough for the roof to be used as a terrace in summer and for the storage of tools, grain and firewood (a reason for the frequent fires in Egyptian villages). The house itself has two or three dank, ill-lit rooms, where the family sleeps for most of the year with its animals. The *fellahin* women are expected to do very little. They rarely help in the fields, and the family meals require little cooking or preparation. The dust and mud make cleanliness difficult, but they do not attempt to sweep or to tidy their houses, while the children are commonly filthy and covered with flies. The Nubian villages are very much cleaner in comparison.

The women do little housework, but they do nothing else. In contrast with North Africans, and still more with the Indian peasants of North and South America, they do not sew, embroider or make pottery. An effort is now being made by the Ministry of Social Affairs to start domestic industries and crafts in the villages, but after centuries of neglect these are difficult to revive.

The creators of Egypt's wealth, the *fellahin* have been oppressed, neglected and despised for so long that it is not surprising that they have become submissive and fatalistic. What they need is the opportunity to display the skill, experience and perseverance which make them potentially some of the best farmers in the world. Any agrarian reform programme in Egypt has to have this end in view.

AGRARIAN REFORM

As we have seen, the foremost aim of the land reform measures decreed by the revolutionary leaders was frankly political. The officers believed that the large landowners were blocking any effective reforms in Egypt through their ability to influence elections in the countryside and so control parliament. The second objective was to alleviate the conditions of small land-owners and landless agricultural workers; but, as we shall see, legislation in itself was able to achieve little in this direction.

The main provision of the first land reform, therefore, was to limit the size of properties to 200 *feddans*. Exceptions were allowed for companies owning land under reclamation for purposes of sale; private individuals owning and reclaiming desert land, which would be exempt from expropriation for twenty-five years; and industrial concerns and agricultural societies. At the same time family *waqfs* (or entails which vested the usufruct of the land in the heirs for ever) were abolished and the properties divided among the beneficiaries. Landowners were also allowed to transfer ownership of fifty *feddans* to each of not more than two children. In 1958 a maximum of 300 *feddans* for family holdings was decreed, and in July 1961, as part of the series of socialist measures, this was further reduced to 100 *feddans*.

In some areas of Egypt families have succeeded in retaining a degree of their influence by a judicious distribution of owner-ship among different branches of the family. But the influence is now localized; it does not extend to the government or, except in minor measure, to the National Assembly. On the other hand, it cannot be said that any of the large landowners have suffered anything approaching destitution. The law of 9 September 1952 permitted private sales of land due for expropria-tion in lots not exceeding five *feddans* to farmers owning less than that amount. There was a rush to sell (though the provision that sales should only be made to small farmers was widely evaded) and the price of land fell by fifty per cent. Further sales were prohibited on 31 October, but by then at least 150,000 *feddans* had been sold. After the second land reform of 1961, landowners were allowed until 1970 to sell any land that they held in excess of 100 *feddans*.

Under the 1952 law, landowners were to receive compensa-tion in non-negotiable three per cent government bonds re-deemable in thirty years at the rate of ten times the estimated rental value of the land, which was calculated as seven times the land tax before the reform was decreed. This has worked out to an average of slightly less than £E. 200 a *feddan*, which means that an expropriated landlord received £E. 6 a year for every *feddan* taken from him by the reform. Under the 1961 law compensation was made payable in fifteen-year four per cent negotiable bonds. Altogether, the two land reforms have achieved a significant though not very radical redistribution of income from the rich to the poor.

Redistribution of expropriated land takes time, because the Agrarian Reform Authority tries to ensure that it is done equitably. Preference is given to former tenants who own less than five *feddans* themselves and to permanent labourers, while the size of the holdings granted varies between two and three *feddans* according to the size of the family. In 1962, the government decided to expropriate, with compensation, all agricultural land owned by foreigners, and this will ultimately provide about another 140,000 *feddans* for redistribution. When, after a few more years, all the land expropriated from Egyptians and foreigners under the first and second land reforms has been redistributed, it will amount to about one million *feddans* or seventeen per cent of the total cultivated area, and it will have benefited about 250,000 families or about eight per cent of the *fellahin*.

The very large estates have disappeared, the middle class (15–20 *feddans*) and upper middle class (20–100 *feddans*) estates have remained untouched, while there has been an increase of a few per cent in the number of holdings of less than five *feddans*. The general pattern of Egyptian land ownership, with the vast majority consisting of very small properties, has not changed.

It was originally intended that the 1952 land reform should be self-financing. The beneficiaries were to pay the expropriated landlords in instalments over thirty years together with three per cent interest and fifteen per cent for the costs of administration. In fact, because the 178,000 acres owned by the royal family were expropriated without compensation but still paid for by the beneficiaries on the same terms as the other redistributed lands, the State was making a handsome profit out of the operation in the first years. In 1961, however, payment by the beneficiaries themselves was reduced to half the total amount paid as compensation to the owners, the period was extended from thirty years to forty, and the interest was halved to 1.5 per cent. The State made itself liable for the difference, and this will amount to more than £E. 50 million by the time the operation is completed.

The instalments paid by the new owners of land invariably came to less than the rent they had paid as tenants. In his *Land Reform in Italy and Egypt*, published in 1956, Sir Malcolm Darling estimated the average increase in net income as fifty per cent, and this figure has been accepted by other independent experts. In general the *fellahin* in Upper Egypt gained most, because rents there had been much higher than in Lower Egypt.

As we have seen, the redistribution of expropriated land will at most have benefited eight per cent of the *fellahin* when it is completed. Article 3 of the 1952 law, which decreed compulsory reduction of all agricultural rents, benefited many more – perhaps four million of the farming population. The new rents were calculated on the same principle as compensation for the expropriated landlords – they were not allowed to exceed seven times the basic land tax – and in the case of sharecropping rents, the owner's portion was not to exceed one half of the yield after deduction of all expenses. These measures also provided the beneficiaries with an average net increase in income of about fifty per cent. Tenants, moreover, were given increased security of contract, which reduced their constant fear of eviction. The 1952 law decreed that all new leases were to be made in writing and were to cover at least three years. All existing tenancy contracts were extended for another year, and since then two extension periods of three years each have been provided for half the area of leased land.

Those who benefited least from the reform were the agricultural labourers and casual workers. It is true that a statutory minimum wage rate of eighteen piastres (about 3s.) a day for men and ten piastres (about 1s. 10d.) for others was decreed, but because of the large surplus of unemployed these measures were unenforceable. At first agricultural labourers were actually worse off, since the break-up of the large estates caused a sharp

reduction in demand for their labour; but later they were re-
cruited in large numbers for work on new land reclamation
projects, the High Dam and canal building connected with it,
and industrial construction.

In 1956 it was possible to say of the reduction in rents that
'this improvement in income and legal status for a very large
section of the farm population is by far the most valuable
achievement of the reform, greatly exceeding in importance the
benefits of redistribution'. (Doreen Warriner, *Land Reform and
Development in the Middle East.*) Unfortunately, much of this
achievement was only temporary. When Miss Warriner returned
to Egypt in early 1961, she found that 'as landowners have now
recovered from the initial shock, there is at present much evasion
of the provisions controlling rent'. Not all was lost, because the
tenants still had better security of tenure for at least half of
their land, and legal rents were enforced by the cooperatives
wherever these had undertaken to collect the rent themselves
from the tenant and pay it to the landlord. But in general
nothing had been able to prevent the overwhelming pressure of
demand for a limited supply of agricultural land from forcing
rents and the price of land upwards, even to above their levels
before the Revolution.

Must we therefore conclude that agrarian reform in Egypt
has been a failure because it has been defeated by the realities
of the Egyptian economy? This is not the case, because the
results achieved by the Agrarian Reform Authority *in the areas
directly under its control* have pointed the way for the rest of the
country.

THE SUPERVISED COOPERATIVES

Wherever small farmers acquired new land under the agrarian
reform, special cooperatives were established, and these differ
in many important respects from the ordinary agricultural cooperatives in the rest of the country, which are mainly concerned
with credit and supply. Membership of the Agrarian Reform
cooperatives was made compulsory. They advance loans to
members and provide them with seed, fertilizers, livestock, and

agricultural machinery, together with storage and transport of crops. Under the first Agrarian Reform decree, they were charged with undertaking the organization of cultivation 'in the most efficient manner including selection, varieties of crops, pest-control and the maintenance and improvement of irrigation'. They also sold all the main crops for the members after deducting instalments for the purchase price of the land and interest on agricultural and other loans.

These supervised cooperatives have been a striking success. In general they have been well and honestly administered under the supervision of the Ministry of Social Affairs and the Ministry of Agrarian Reform, and crop yields, especially of cotton, have risen sharply. Total cotton output by supervised cooperatives in sixteen districts increased by forty-five per cent between 1952 and 1959, compared with fifteen per cent in the rest of the country. Increases for sugar and other crops were not as high, but they were undoubtedly above the national average.

The technical advantage of the supervised cooperatives lies in their ability to use large-scale farming methods for small properties. All the land in the village is divided into large fields, each several hundred *feddans* in size and raising a single crop. The beneficiaries of the reform are then allotted a holding in three pieces with each in a different field, so that one will be under cotton, another under maize or rice, and the third under berseem (Egyptian clover). The advantage in being able to plough, irrigate, and spray with pesticide such large areas is obvious. The triennial rotation was made compulsory for all the land reform areas in 1956. Elsewhere the *fellahin* normally used a biennial rotation, as follows:

November – May: wheat or berseem (Egyptian clover).

June – July: fallow.

August – November: maize, millet or rice.

December – January: fallow or berseem.

February – November: cotton.

This produced at least three crops every two years, but it exhausted the soil. Where some progressive large landowners used a triennial rotation, yields were up to twenty per cent higher. The success of the triennial rotation in the land reform areas caused the government to make it compulsory throughout the country by Law No. 166 of 1963.

Significant social advances are registered by the supervised cooperatives because most of the profits made by them are saved or invested. One of the biggest problems of the Egyptian countryside is that if the *fellah* has a good year, he immediately spends the windfall on a new wife or in marrying off his daughter. In the reform cooperatives dividends are small, reserves are accumulated as insurance against a drop in cotton prices, and the rest of the profits are spent on socially useful purposes. In one that the author visited a new mosque, a clinic (with permanent doctor and nurse), and a social centre (with television set) had all been purchased out of profits. The houses, shops and appearance of the peasants were all well above the average in Delta villages.

In many ways supervised cooperatives are a severe restriction on the individual liberties of the peasant farmers. They go at least half-way towards collectivization or nationalization of the land. But Egypt's agricultural situation is such that no reasonable alternative really exists between controlled or supervised cooperatives and communal farms on the Chinese pattern. Voluntary cooperatives of the kind that exist elsewhere in Egypt have shown that they cannot prevent the small landowners from sinking steadily deeper into debt. They are usually dominated by a small group of the larger landlords who use them for their own benefit.

The government has accordingly decided to extend the system of supervised cooperatives by degrees all over the country. Because it is to be done gradually, this has received little publicity, but it amounts to nothing less than an agricultural revolution. If it is to be a success, it cannot be imposed on the *fellahin* against their wishes; but fortunately there is a precedent in one village outside the land reform area where the *fellahin* were won over by the obvious advantages of the scheme. The village of Nawag near Tanta in the Delta was chosen because there fragmentation of holdings had gone to extreme lengths. In a total area of 1,850 *feddans*, there were 1,585 properties and 3,500 plots, each with different drainage and irrigation schemes.

The villagers were asked to accept the division of their village into several large fields, each of which – as in the supervised cooperatives – would be under one crop. They were not asked to consolidate their holdings, or alter the pattern of ownership in any way; but like all peasants, they were cautious and they first agreed only to try the experiment on a hundred *feddans*. This was such a success that the next year they agreed to extend the scheme to the whole village. A similar experiment at Minshat Sultan, a larger village in the Menufia province, has been equally successful.

At the end of 1960 the government decided in principle to extend the system of supervised cooperatives to all other agricultural cooperative societies. But nothing much more was done until 1963, when it was decided to begin in two governorates – Beni Suef in Upper Egypt and Kafr el-Sheikh in the Delta. The farmers are being persuaded to accept *tagmi'a* of their holdings (or the grouping into several large fields). The two governorates have been divided into cooperative districts with a Land Reform representative in each, and for each 1,500 *feddans* there is an inspector with two assistants who deal with an area small enough to permit personal relationships with the *fellahin*. All the land reform officials with whom the author spoke agreed that, however much they would like to have been able to insist on the consolidation of fragmented holdings, it would be fatal to force the pace. One described their method of work as 'slow penetration rather than sudden invasion'.

The extension of *tagmi'a* and supervised cooperatives throughout the country should not imply that before the scheme was begun nothing had been done for rural development apart from the rather moderately successful attempt to reduce rents and raise agricultural labourer's wages. As already mentioned, the *fellahin* have benefited substantially from new schools, rural health centres and clean drinking water. There have been three other lines of attack on rural poverty and social backwardness:

The Gamoos *(buffalo) scheme.* For work and as a milk producer, the buffalo is invaluable to all small Egyptian farmers;

indeed it produces an annual net income equal to that of one *feddan*. In 1958 a Presidential decree provided for the distribution of animals to all *fellahin* without livestock at very reduced prices, with the money payable in instalments over four years.

The Rural Credit Scheme. This was launched in 1957 by the Ministry of Social Affairs and the Agricultural and Co-operative Credit Bank (which was founded in 1931). Its purpose was to help tenant farmers, who now constitute a substantial majority of the *fellahin*, by allowing the Bank to make loans on the security of crops instead of only the land. The interest rate was not to exceed three per cent, and the crops themselves were to be marketed through the cooperatives.

The Combined Units. The idea of combined rural social centres to provide health, educational, agricultural and social services to the population of the countryside was initiated in 1938 by a voluntary body. In 1940 the new Ministry of Social Affairs took over the work, and by 1955 there were 185 of these centres in existence across Egypt with each one serving about 10,000 people. Each centre had an agricultural advisor, who was also a social worker, a doctor, a nurse-midwife and a laboratory assistant. In 1954 it was decided to recast and extend the whole scheme. The Ministries of Agriculture and Education were brought in, and the centres were expanded to include sections for hygiene, education, social affairs and agriculture, and to serve 15,000 people each. By the end of 1964 there were 300 of these serving nearly five million, and the aim has been set to raise the number to 868 and so cover the whole rural population. The villagers contribute two *feddans* of land and £E. 1,500 towards each centre. The health and social workers are carefully selected and trained and are supposed to live in a manner as similar as possible to the villagers themselves. The *fellahin* themselves are generally very well disposed towards the centres, although they tend to be more attracted by their health and welfare services than by the economic and technical advice that they are intended to provide. Shortage of money and suitable staff has prevented the system from being expanded more rapidly. It is an imaginative, idealistic but at the same time practical idea, which could do more than anything to regenerate the Egyptian countryside. The low white building of the combined centres standing close to the unfired mud bricks of the village houses provides something like a symbol of hope for the future.

EXTENDING THE CULTIVATED AREA

Egypt is as big as France and Spain together, but its cultivated and inhabited area is about the size of Holland. When Muhammad Aly came to power, the cultivated area comprised some two million *feddans*, and through the building of dams and the improvement of irrigation during the nineteenth and early twentieth centuries this was raised to nearly six million *feddans* by the First World War. Today it stands at only slightly more than this figure, although the crop area has been increased to about eleven million *feddans* by the change-over from basin to perennial irrigation. When the High Dam is completed almost all the remaining 900,000 *feddans* which are still under basin irrigation will be changed over to perennial, and the only way to increase the crop area will be by reclaiming new land from the desert.

When the High Dam reaches its full storage capacity of 130,000 million cubic metres of water, it will be possible to reclaim between 1,000,000 and 1,200,000 *feddans* in Upper Egypt and on the fringes of the Delta. Through the use of subterranean water and improved drainage (much of the Delta land is at present overwatered) it will thus be possible to increase the total cultivated area to 7,700,000 feddans. According to one expert (H. E. Hurst in *The Nile*) this is the absolute maximum that can be irrigated in Egypt from the waters of the Nile (especially if future developments in the Sudan are taken into consideration). Some Egyptian experts, however, are more optimistic. Dr Muhammad Ibrahim Hassan forecast in *al-Ahram* (12 January 1965) that it would be possible to increase the cultivated area to ten million *feddans* – by draining half the area of the five great shallow lakes of the northern Delta (leaving the other half for fishing), so as to produce about half a million *feddans*; and by using cheap power from the High Dam to bring water to desert lands within twenty metres of the river level, so as to reclaim a further two million *feddans*.

Time will show whether this estimate is over-optimistic, and meanwhile several important reclamation schemes are progressing in different parts of the country. Reclamation by large land-owners or private companies naturally ceased after the land reform, and all schemes are now planned and supervised by two bodies – the General Egyptian Organization for Land Reclamation and the General Egyptian Organization for Desert Reclamation.

Among the reclamation projects that are actually under way are those in the Fayum Oasis and at Abis near Alexandria (which are being carried out in collaboration with the United States by the Egyptian–American Rural Improvement Service); in the Eastern Delta (in cooperation with the Italian firm Italconsult); in the Kom Ombo Valley in Upper Egypt where the 50,000 Nubians displaced by the rising waters of Lake Nasser have been resettled; in the Wadi Natrun, in the western part of the Sinai Peninsula, to which Nile water has been piped under the Suez Canal from the Delta; and along the north-west Mediterranean coast near Mersa Matruh. Part of the new Soviet–Egyptian economic agreement which was first mentioned at the end of Mr Khrushchev's visit to Egypt in May 1964 and confirmed by Soviet Deputy Premier Shelepin at Cairo in December, was that the U.S.S.R. would cooperate with Egypt in reclaiming 200,000 *feddans* of desert land.

These are not all the current reclamation schemes, and there are two more of special interest. One is the Tahrir (Liberation) Province to the west of the Delta, which was established after the Revolution, as part of the first land reform, with the aim of creating a new type of farming community. The land was owned collectively, the settlers were carefully selected, and trained social workers attempted to recondition their lives. But this idealistic experiment was enormously expensive, and after an outcry in the National Assembly in 1957 it was scaled down and the reclaimed land divided among the settler families.

Now it is more economic but little different from any other reclamation scheme, except that the settlers receive more land and higher wages than elsewhere.

The other project is the New Valley, which is of outstanding interest because it will ultimately change the ancient face of Egypt entirely. When this scheme was started in 1960, geologists knew that there was a lot of water in the Western Desert under the five oases of Kharga, Dakhla, Farafra, Bahriyah and Siwa; but they did not know whether it was a finite static lake or an underground river. After exhaustive hydrological and geological tests, they became reasonably certain that it was something like a river which emerged from the Tebasti Mountains of Chad and the highlands of Western Sudan – where there is heavy annual rainfall – and which seeped northwards through the Nubian sandstone at a speed of some twenty-seven metres a year. Work was started in the two southern oases, Kharga and Dakhla, and all the 200 wells that were drilled produced water – sometimes as much as 12,000 cubic metres a day, or enough to irrigate 600 *feddans*. So far about 50,000 *feddans* have been reclaimed, or enough to distribute five *feddans* to each family of oasis-dwellers and to bring in 2,000 new settlers from the Nile Valley near Assiut.

The five oases lie in depressions, and the eventual aim is to reclaim enough land for them to form an almost continuous stretch of green a few miles wide roughly parallel to the Nile Valley. Already a good road has been built linking Assiut with Kharga, Dakhla and Farafra. When this has been completed through Bahriyah to Siwa and the Mediterranean coast, the Nile Valley and the Red Sea will no longer be the only north–south links in the country. From the pharaonic, Persian, Greek, and Roman remains in the Western Desert it is known that this area was much more prosperous and inhabited than it is today with its population of 60,000. At their height the Western Desert oases may have supported half a million people, and if modern towns with industries can take root there, the population can one day be even larger than that.

About two hundred miles to the south of Kharga lies another great depression which is entirely desert, and the Desert

Reclamation Organization is at present considering the possibility of irrigating this from Lake Nasser. If the lands turn out suitable for reclamation, it may be possible to cultivate an immense area of 2,000,000 *feddans* by building a short canal from the lake near the Sudanese border and irrigating by gravity. It may also be feasible to cultivate several hundred thousand *feddans* in two valleys which will reach the eastern shore of the lake when this has filled up. Some Egyptians have even expressed the hope that the Nubians will one day be able to return and settle on the shores of Lake Nasser. These may be distant dreams, but they are far from impossible.

CONCLUSION

Redistribution of ownership, reduction of rents, increased wages, semi-collectivization (or supervised cooperatives), rural development (combined centres, clinics, schools, clean water) and reclamation of marsh and desert lands are the methods which have and are being used to tackle Egypt's fundamental problem – the miserable social and economic conditions of the people who live on the land. The question is whether they are enough or whether we must agree with Egyptian Marxist writers like Hassan Riad, that 'there is no solution to the problem of Egyptian rural society within the agricultural sector' (*L'Egypte Nassérienne*, p. 35).

Not everyone who has studied the problem is equally pessimistic. Marxists tend to paint an excessively sombre picture of the present because they see the only hope for the future in a 'Chinese solution' where the state, in Hassan Riad's words, 'mobilizes the hidden productive forces of the mass of the people' and 'invests human beings rather than capital'.

Non-Marxists such as Gabriel Saab (described somewhat tendentiously as a 'classical economist' by another Egyptian Marxist, Anwar Abdul Malek in *Egypte Société Militaire*, p. 84), are more optimistic. Saab points out that although yields per acre of cotton, wheat, rice, and sugar can be increased very little in Egypt because they are so high already, a very substantial increase in profit per acre could be achieved by switching land to fruit, vegetables, meat, and dairy production. It is obviously wasteful that Egypt's intensely fertile but precious agricultural land should be used to grow cereals and rice, the cultivation of which uses an excessive amount of water. Egypt already grows most of the Mediterranean vegetables and fruits and some tropical ones (like mangoes) as well as roses, gladioli and other flowers. By concentrating more on these, it could build up an export trade to Europe and the other Arab States in winter and early spring. At the same time, by mechanization and by reducing the area under cereals and rice, it could dispense with many of the draft animals, eliminate some of the enormous area used for growing fodder, and concentrate on meat and dairy produce. Gabriel Saab believes that even with mechanization this kind of highly intensive mixed farming would employ more rather than less labour. Undoubtedly it would increase profits per acre several times. Of all the main crops which Egypt grows at present, only cotton – for which the country has a high reputation and special advantages – would remain, at least as long as the world demand for Egyptian extra and medium long staples is maintained.

Intensification of Egyptian agriculture, combined with reclamation of new land and a crash programme of industrialization offer some hope of a solution. The limiting factors are time and money, which in this case amount to the same thing. The conversion of land from the cultivation of cereals and rice to fruit, vegetables and flowers, and the development of meat and dairy farming require heavy capital investment. The *fellahin* have to be retrained in new farming techniques, for the packing and exporting of market garden produce demand a much higher level of skill than the export of cereals, and orchards take several years before they show a profit. Land reclamation is also a skilled and costly business. In the New Valley, for instance, where all the economic infrastructure of roads, electric power, drains, etc. had to be created first, reclamation costs about £E. 350 a *feddan*. By the end of the first Five-Year Plan in June 1965, about 520,000 *feddans* will have been reclaimed in the Valley and Delta, as well as 203,000 *feddans* of desert land. After that the programme is to reclaim about 150,000 *feddans* annually, which is the most that can be done with the available technical and capital reserves.

THE HIGH DAM

The High Dam is the core and mainstay of the two Five-Year Plans. Regarded solely as a means of increasing the crop area by about twenty-five per cent, it obviously can provide no more than a breathing-space, for the rising population will swallow up the extra land in less than ten years. But it is intended to do very much more than this. The official estimate of the increase in the national income that it will produce is as follows:

	£E. (*million*)
1. Increasing the present cultivated area by about one million *feddans* and converting 700,000 *feddans* in Upper Egypt from basin to perennial irrigation	63
2. Guaranteeing water requirements for crops even in years of low flood, improving drainage, and guaranteeing the cultivation of one million *feddans* of rice annually	56
3. Protecting the country against the dangers of high flood, preventing seepage and the inundation of small islands and river banks	10
4. Improving navigation conditions on the Nile	5
5. Producing electric power annually of about 10 thousand million kwh	100
Total:	234

Since the total cost of the High Dam – including the hydro-electric scheme and the building of canals, drains, roads, etc. – is estimated at £E. 404 million, this means that the Dam should amortize itself in less than two years. This seems to be over-optimistic; the Dam is likely to cost more than the estimate, and no calculation has been made for the loss of the fertilizing Nile silt which will be held behind in Lake Nasser and will have to be replaced by extra fertilizers because the canal and drain building will take several years to complete.

On the other hand, after the super-human effort in early 1964 to finish the first stage on schedule for Mr Khrushchev's visit in May, it now looks as if the programme is as much as a year ahead, and the first hydro-electric power will be produced in 1966 instead of 1967 as originally planned. Finally, the training of Egyptian engineers and technicians (welders, crane-drivers, etc.) as well as the experience of managing a vast enterprise that employs more than 30,000 men will be of inestimable value to Egypt. When the High Dam is finished, Egypt will be in a position to tender for the construction of dams in other countries.

Electric energy production per head in Egypt has quadrupled since the Revolution. The High Dam, through increasing the output of existing hydro-electric power stations on the Nile as well as through what it will produce itself, will triple the output again to 16.5 billion kwh or 525 kwh per head (compared with the world average of 600 kwh). The hope of the High Dam is not that it will 'solve Egypt's economic problems'; no reasonably informed person ever believed it would. What it could do is jolt the economy on to a slightly higher level, from which it might attain Professor Rostow's 'take-off'. The cheap electric power should help Egyptian industry to expand more rapidly and to become more competitive. The increased incomes of the rapidly increasing numbers of industrial workers in the towns should enable them to pay more for the food produced by the *fellahin* who, at least for a few years, will have substantially more land per head to cultivate. If this is accompanied, as it certainly will be, by a frontal attack on the ignorance and social backwardness of the *fellahin*, it is possible to foresee the creation of a new atmosphere and outlook in the Egyptian countryside.

Egypt's social and economic problems are so daunting that some people have come to regard the country as a hopeless case – doomed to remain one of the slum quarters of the world. It is not necessary to be as pessimistic as this. In its struggle to overcome the poverty and ignorance of its people, Egypt has two great assets. Its population has been confined for several thousand years to the Valley and Delta of the Nile, dependent upon the river for its livelihood, and though this has caused its poverty and overcrowding, it has also made it cohesive and amenable to strong central government – far more so, indeed, than most other under-developed nations. For a country which has to mobilize all its resources in a frontal offensive on its economic problems, this is a priceless advantage.

The other asset is the ninety-six per cent of its territory which at present is unexploited desert. With the progress of technology there are scores of possible ways in which Egypt may be able to make use of this land. Apart from reclamation for agriculture, there is a strong possibility that the deserts contain minerals which have yet to be discovered, since only a small part of them has yet been surveyed. Coal has recently been found in commercial quantities in Central Sinai, and big deposits of iron ore, one in the Bahriyah oasis, discovered. Uranium, copper, zinc, manganese, sulphur, asbestos, and gold are all either being mined already or have been found. The best prospects for crude oil production still seem to be along the Red Sea coasts and off-shore, although there is the possibility of a strike by the companies now searching the Western Desert. Dr Sidqi, the Deputy Prime Minister for Industry and Mining, has said that he expects Egypt to be producing twelve million tons a year by 1970, which would make it a net exporter of oil.

The Qattara depression scheme, which is still being surveyed, would bring the Mediterranean into the depression to produce immense quantities of cheap electricity for irrigation pumps and industry. Finally there is the strong possibility of a breakthrough in research on the distillation of sea water for agriculture, a discovery that would at once transform Egypt's economic prospects since the country has vast areas of good soil covered only by a thin layer of sand.

Emigration has never seriously been considered as a solution of Egypt's problems, because there is no country that would accept the *fellahin* in any numbers or where they could be persuaded to go. The only possible exception is the Sudan, and even this presents political difficulties that are probably insuperable. But emigration within Egypt's borders, from the Valley into the desert, is something that can be foreseen if some or all the possibilities for exploiting desert regions are achieved. For the Egyptian people even this will not be easy, since most of them dislike leaving the Valley for any length of time. But ultimately it provides the great hope of creating a prosperous and dynamic nation.

11 The Search for a Political System

First. Political democracy cannot be separated from social democracy. No citizen can be regarded as free to vote unless he is given the following three guarantees:

1. he should be free from exploitation in all its forms;
2. he should have an equal opportunity with his fellow citizen to enjoy a fair share of the national wealth;
3. his mind should be free from all anxiety likely to undermine his future security.

Second. Political democracy cannot exist under the domination of any one class. Democracy means, literally, the domination and sovereignty of the people – the whole people.

(*National Charter*, Chapter 5.)

These are high ideals for any country, but especially for one which has long been a by-word for exploitation, class dominance, and grossly unequal opportunity. The revolutionary regime has set itself the double task of redistributing power, wealth, and influence among the Egyptian people and of increasing the national income enough for each citizen to lead a decent life. The social and economic obstacles to doing this in Egypt would in any case be immense; but Nasser, with the approval of his government and the great majority of the Egyptian people, has specifically rejected two methods of approach which have been tried with some degree of success in other countries. One is liberal capitalism, through which the major Western European powers and the United States achieved their first industrial revolutions in the nineteenth century. In all of these countries an increasingly prosperous bourgeoisie provided the savings and capital for new economic advances, while a politically feeble industrial working class was unable to press its demands for a larger share of the national wealth. By the time this class had gained some power in the twentieth century, these countries were so far ahead in the economic race that they could afford a substantial redistribution of income. Nasser is no doubt right in believing that any such course of development would be impossible for Egypt in the mid twentieth century, even if he thought it desirable (which he does not). The workers of all countries have learned too much from the experience of those in the pioneer industrial States.

The other system which the Egyptian revolution has rejected is Marxist–Leninism or, more specifically, Soviet Stalinism of the 1930s and 1940s and Chinese Communism of the 1950s and 1960s. Neither of these is a meaningless proposition for Egypt. In both cases an all-powerful state machine working through a centralized Communist Party has achieved spectacular economic advances by mobilizing and regimenting the country's resources of labour and capital. While the Russian and Chinese people have both suffered severely from the deliberate holding down of consumption, the governments of both countries have been able to use the enforced savings to establish a solid base of heavy industry. The Russians have progressed further because they began thirty years earlier; but the Chinese have used Soviet experience to avoid some of the Soviet Union's mistakes. In particular their agricultural policy seems to have been more successful than that of the Russians.

Except for the period of the 'Iraqi crisis' in 1959, Egypt has generally had good relations with the Communist States since it adopted a non-aligned policy in 1954–5. But Nasser has never wavered in his belief that a Communist system is inapplicable to Egypt itself. His attitude to Marxism has softened during the years. In a preface he wrote in early 1955 to a violent anti-Communist tract entitled 'The Reality of Communism', he accused the Communists of having rejected personal liberty and equality to create an unjust pyramidal social organization dominated by a single individual. Since then he has accepted and absorbed into his own thinking a large part of Marxist teaching on society and relations between the classes. But his fundamental objections remain. As he said in an interview with the London *Sunday Times* in June 1962, when describing his years as a student:

I was approached on several occasions to join the Communist Party, but although I studied Marxist doctrine and the works of Lenin with sympathy, I encountered two basic obstacles, ones that I knew could never be overcome. First, Communism is in its essence atheistic; I have always been a sincere Moslem with an unshakeable belief in an outside force that we call God who watches over all our destinies. It is quite impossible to be a good Moslem and a good Communist. Second, I realized that Communism necessitated certain control from Moscow and the central Communist Parties, and this, too, I could never accept.

For these reasons, the small Egyptian Communist Party has never been allowed to act as the spearhead of the revolutionary movement. Since it was hopelessly divided and included a high proportion of Christians and Jews (many of them with foreign nationality) among its leaders, it is unlikely that it could have undertaken the role even if it had been offered it. But throughout the vital years 1958–63, it was vigorously suppressed and its prominent members imprisoned. At the same time, no other political parties have been permitted. The young revolutionary officers took a few years to reject liberal economic principles, but they were convinced from the very beginning that Egypt could not progress under a Western type of parliamentary constitution. Such a democracy was a sham façade in their view, because 'it is an indisputable fact that the political system in any state is only a reflection of the interests controlling the economic system'. (*National Charter*, Chapter 4.) Since an alliance of 'feudalism and exploiting capitalism' controlled the economy, it also controlled the political parties and parliament. In the villages the feudalists had the power to order the *fellahin* how to vote; in the towns, the capitalists bribed the voters. And if both these methods failed, the ruling classes resorted to simple fraud.

It would be hard to argue with this analysis, at least from Egypt's experience. If Neguib had won in 1954 and the old parties and constitution had been restored, there can be no doubt that elections would have brought to power most of the same men as before. There would have been no land reform or any other serious attempt to alter the social system.

Nasser was convinced that before the country was ready to be governed by elected representative institutions, a system had to be devised to ensure that these would never be dominated by the exploiting classes, who would try to reverse the achievements of the Revolution. He came to the conclusion that even the limited powers given to the National Assembly (which was elected in June 1957 and was dissolved after the union with Syria in 1958) and the National Union (which became the single political organization for the United Arab Republic between 1958 and 1961) were premature, because the reactionaries succeeded in infiltrating them. For the first twelve years of the Revolution, therefore, Nasser virtually governed without any means of consulting the popular will.

At the same time he had no cadre of revolutionary theorists and militants to lead the revolution from the top. When they seized power, the Free Officers were a secret association within the army dedicated to the overthrow of the monarchy. There was no Egyptian party or organization representing the revolution to compare with the F.L.N. in Algeria, the Neo-Destour in Tunisia or, still less, the Indian Congress Party. The nearest Egyptian equivalent was the Wafd, but it was partly *against* the Wafd and all it represented that the military *coup* was promoted. The Egyptian Communist Party and Marxist intellectuals were prevented from fulfilling the role. In 1964 it could be said that Nasser had been the sole theoretician and executive of the Egyptian Revolution. He was certainly aware of the drawbacks in this situation; in the early 1960s, he often referred in private and public to the dangers of relying too heavily on one man. The assassination of President Kennedy and the death of Mr Nehru caused everyone in Egypt to pause and consider what would happen if Gamal Abdul Nasser was suddenly removed from the scene.

To some extent the devolution of the presidential powers to popular institutions was prevented by events. The first attempt to give Nasser's powers a constitutional basis was made in the constitution published in January 1956. This provided for a national plebiscite to be held on the constitution and on Nasser's candidature for the presidency. In both cases ninety-nine per cent of the electorate voted 'yes'. The Revolutionary Command Council ceased to exist, and the President formed a new Cabinet which excluded some of the former R.C.C. members. Article 192 of the 1956 constitution provided for a National Union to re-place all the political parties (and the rather vague Liberation Rally which had been founded soon after the Revolution). But almost immediately after the national plebiscite the Suez crisis intervened, and Nasser was too busy devoting himself to the preservation of Egypt as an independent State to concern himself very much with internal affairs.

The National Union was formally established in May 1957 and played a leading role in the elections to the National Assembly in July 1957. About 2,500 candidates for the 350 Assembly seats were screened by a National Executive Committee, which eliminated nearly half of them, and the Assembly met between July 1957 and March 1958, when it was dissolved because the union with Syria required a reorganization of the political structure. During its brief life, it was widely regarded as a rubber stamp for the government's policies, but this description is not wholly just. It did provide some outlet for public criticism of abuses, and one of its most notable achievements was to call to account the Liberation Province scheme which had been wastefully and corruptly administered.

During 1958 the governmental structure of the United Arab Republic was evolved, to produce a President, four Vice-Presidents, a Central Cabinet and two Regional Councils, one for Syria and one for Egypt. The Syrian political parties dissolved themselves with varying degrees of enthusiasm and sincerity, and the National Union system was applied to both regions of the U.A.R. This system, which was continually being amended during the three and a half years of union, was complicated and confused. The public did not understand it, and it never took root in either region, especially Syria. The trouble was that the union only held together as long as it did because of Nasser's personal prestige in Syria, and throughout the years of union he was much too involved in the day-to-day affairs of government to devote any time to creating a political system suited to Syria's idiosyncrasies. It was difficult enough to do this in Egypt, which he knew and understood.

Syria's secession from the union in September 1961 was a humiliating experience for Nasser, but it provided an invaluable opportunity to consider the mistakes that had been made. Already by 16 October he had reached some conclusions.

Reaction managed to infiltrate into the National Union to paralyse its revolutionary potentialities and turn into a mere organizational façade unstirred by the forces of the masses and their genuine demands. The fact that proved this mistake was that some of those who are in the front ranks of the separatist revolutionary movement in Syria had themselves been in the front rank of the National Union organization. Hence, the most important task that faces us today is to reorganize the National Union to become a revolutionary instrument for the masses, who alone have a rightful interest in the revolutionary changes. The National Union should be for the workers, peasants, educated people, professional men and proprietors whose property is not based on exploitation, for officers and soldiers who were the pioneers of the great Revolution of 23 July, for the genuine owners of wealth, its protectors and defenders, and for those whose hopes socialism has fulfilled.

On 18 October a new government was announced, and on 25 November the so-called Preparatory Committee of the National Congress of Popular Powers met in Cairo. In a long address the President told the Committee that its task was to prepare for a National Congress which would lay down a Charter of National Action to be the basis of the next general elections. The National Congress consisted of 1,750 members elected by labour, professional associations, and other community groups, and it met in May 1962 to hear Nasser present his 30,000-word draft National Charter. There followed a series of televised debates in which the President discussed various aspects of the Charter with the Congress; the discussions were then taken up by the Press and in towns and villages all over the country. It was the most genuine popular debate that the country had known.

The National Congress discussions revealed the tremendous difficulties of creating a vital democratic system in Egypt. Nasser showed impatience as delegate after delegate stood up only to echo his words and praise him. He was obliged to stand firmly against strong pressure to make him president for life.

Finally, on 30 June, the draft National Charter was approved by the Congress unamended in its entirety. The future political structure of Egypt had in fact been decided by one man – Gamal Abdul Nasser – but at least he had been able to devote his mind and energies to the matter during the previous six months. His main aims as he expressed them in his speeches at the time were to guarantee the safety of the Revolution against the reactionary elements in society and to create a 'genuine democracy' (as opposed to the 'sham façade' of pre-revolutionary parliamentary regimes) by associating all the other elements from the grass-roots upwards in the process of government.

It would be untrue to say that nothing had been done towards achieving this aim before. The National Union never gained the confidence or interest of the mass of the people during the five years of its legal existence, but it did establish the framework for the pyramidal system of government which was to become the pattern in the 1960s. With more time and less outside distractions, Nasser and his colleagues might have been able to blow life into it.

One of the main reasons why the public never understood the National Union was that its structure and organization were continually being changed from the time that it was brought into being. Foreign observers had the utmost difficulty in gaining any clear picture of it even from senior Egyptian officials. At the foundation level, the National Union consisted of elected executive committees, containing from three to ten members each in the villages and thirty members each in the more densely populated *qisms* or town quarters. Voting was compulsory for all males over eighteen and optional for women, and elections were actually held for these committees throughout Egypt in November 1959. Each committee elected two men to represent it at the next level of government, the district (*markaz*), and then the governorate (*muhafazat*).

An important part of the National Union idea was that the basic committees should appoint special auxiliary committees from among local citizens to help with social, cultural, and economic projects such as public hygiene, literacy campaigns, and rural industries. In 1960 it was decided to bring the rural combined units into the system of local government by transferring the powers of their councils to the basic committees and at the same time making the executive heads of the units *ex officio* members of the committees.

In 1960 a new local government law was introduced which went a long way towards decentralizing the administration of Egypt. Under it, each of the twenty-four governorates had an executive council which consisted partly of government representatives, partly of active members of the National Union in the governorate capital, and partly of the two representatives from each of the basic committees. These executive councils were given a legal personality and made financially autonomous. They now enjoy a large measure of authority in matters such as public works, education, transport, housing, planning and location of industry, and the use of some development funds. They enable citizens of the provinces to check and criticize plans emanating from the central government.

When the National Charter was approved in May 1962, therefore, some effort had already been made to associate the mass of the people with both the short- and long-term decisions of government. But anyone could see that the system had to be given new vitality. Above all the members of the regime, including the President, had to devote a major part of their energies to making it work. Egypt has such a long tradition of heavily centralized government that any attempt to strengthen local authority is certain to be difficult.

The Arab Socialist Union, which in the National Charter became the country's single political organization, resembled the National Union in most important respects. The basic units were to be formed in villages and towns, but also now in 'republican organizations' like factories, workshops, companies, government ministries, and business firms. This innovation reflected both the advance of industrialization since the establishment of the National Union and, since the series of nationalizations, the control of most business and individual enterprises by the State. Many of these organizations are so large that they include several basic units.

Members of the basic unit elect a twenty-man committee which meets twice monthly and holds office for two years; the members themselves constitute the basic unit conference, which is supposed to meet every four months. As with the National Union organization, each basic unit committee elects two members to represent it at the next level – the district (*markaz*) – and together these elected members form the district conference, which meets twice yearly and itself elects a district council to meet twice monthly.

From each of the district councils two members are elected to represent them at the next level – the governorate – which also has a conference and an elected council. The only difference from the lower levels is that members are elected for four instead of two years. Above the governorates at the national level there is a general Conference of the A.S.U., composed of members of the governorate councils and also representatives of the army, police, womens' associations, and other community groups. This will only meet every two years, but it will elect a general council to meet every six months, and the general council will in turn elect a higher executive committee.

This is the theoretical framework which was published in 1962, but three years later the structure was still not complete. Once again outside events intervened to divert Nasser's attention. Following the Baathist-led *coups* in Iraq and Syria in early 1963, he was deeply involved first in union negotiations and then in his quarrel with the Baath Party, while in the following year he was caught up in an African, a non-aligned, and two Arab summit conferences. Elections for the basic unit committees were held in May 1963, but by February 1965 the councils at the higher levels had not yet been elected and the first general conference of the A.S.U. had not been held. Yet despite everything, the regime had made a determined effort to popularize the principles of the A.S.U. Three Vice-Presidents devoted themselves almost exclusively to A.S.U. affairs during 1963 and 1964: Hussein el-Shafei to its organization in the country as a whole; Zakariya Muhieddin, in Cairo; and Hassan Ibrahim, in Alexandria.

The most important respect in which the A.S.U. differs from the National Union and any other earlier political organization in Egypt is that half the seats on its elected bodies at all levels must be occupied by farmers and workers because, according to the National Charter, they form the majority of the people and have been deprived the longest of their inalienable right to shape and direct their future. A worker is defined as anyone who is a member of a trade-union. A farmer was originally defined as anyone owning less than five *feddans*; but during the campaign for elections to the National Assembly this qualification was raised to twenty-five *feddans*, which means that it includes the middle-class farmers while still excluding all the former big landowners (who now have 100 *feddans* each).

Another theoretical innovation of the A.S.U. has not yet been put into practice – the distinction between active and associate members. Originally it was intended that while all members could vote in elections, only active members could stand for office. In fact the distinction has never been made, and although it may be introduced later, it is difficult to see how this can be done. There are now about five million members of the A.S.U.; all those applying for membership have been accepted except for those who were subject to sequestration and nationalization laws and so to political 'isolation'. Membership subscription is two piastres (about 4d.) a month, and this is deducted at source from wages and salaries.

THE NATIONAL ASSEMBLY

In November 1963, after a long summer in which it had seemed for a time that Egypt was about to enter into a constitutional union with Syria and Iraq and so have to modify its own political structure, new laws were announced providing for the election in February 1964 of a 350-member National Assembly. There were to be 175 constituencies with each represented by two members, at least one of whom had to be a 'worker or farmer'. All candidates had to be over thirty years of age, able to read and write, and be members of the A.S.U. Members, who could not be civil servants or members of local councils, would be paid £E. 75 a month, and the Assembly would convene every November for at least seven months. The general elections were delayed one month and finally took place on 10 March, with about 1,750 candidates standing for the 350 seats. Of these 993 were workers or farmers (according to the new definitions) and twenty-eight were women.

According to the electoral law, a candidate had to gain an absolute majority over the others in his constituency, and only 108 members were declared elected, because in the remaining constituencies either no one had achieved an absolute majority or no worker and farmer had secured election. A second round was therefore held on 19 March, in which candidates only needed a simple majority of not less than twenty per cent of the registered votes. After the final count it appeared that more than half the members of the Assembly were workers and farmers, while eight were women. Before it convened the President appointed ten more members, bringing the total to 360 (mainly, it is thought, to increase the representation of Copts in the Assembly which was lower than their proportion in the country as a whole). Those elected included Anwar el-Sadat (who was later elected Speaker); Sayed Marei, the former Minister of Agriculture; Mahmoud Yunes, Chairman of the Suez Canal Authority, and Khaled Muhieddin. But a very high proportion of the rest – especially among the workers and farmers – were quite unknown to the public.

Interest in the elections varied in different parts of the country, but in many places electoral meetings were lively and well attended. Since it was strictly forbidden for candidates to adopt any party labels of any kind, they naturally tended to concentrate on local issues. Corruption was certainly not unknown, but there was much less of it than in any previous election, both because of the severe penalties involved and because no candidate thought it worth his while to pay out large sums in order to get elected. This was partly a reflection of a less corrupt atmosphere in public life, but also of uncertainty over what the Assembly's real power and authority would be.

Voting was compulsory with a penalty of £E. 1 for failure to do so. There were widespread complaints that the electoral registers had not been brought up to date; the electoral cards that were used were the same issued in 1957, and many had been lost or destroyed. Some electors, especially in the towns, went to the polls only to avoid the fine. If they did not know the candidates personally, they had no party label to guide them and therefore made their choice at random. Despite all the government's efforts, the electors insisted in some constituencies on voting for representatives of the old regime like a member of the local dominant family. In one provincial town, for instance, a rather unpopular Governor pushed the candidature of a highly intelligent progressive-minded lady lawyer. The public responded by electing an elderly conservative local figure by an overwhelming majority.

The Assembly convened on 26 March 1964. On the previous day, the government was entirely reorganized. Aly Sabry, who had been Chairman of a twenty-four-member Executive Council since it was formed in September 1962, became Prime Minister and Minister of Planning, to head a Cabinet composed of eleven Deputy Prime Ministers, twenty-two Ministers and three Deputies. Mahmoud Fawzi became Deputy Prime Minister of Foreign Affairs; and Hussein Khallaf, Minister of Foreign Culture. Dr Kaissouny became Deputy Prime Minister for Finance and Economy, but he also remained Minister of Economy and Foreign Trade with only a Minister of the Treasury under him.

The Presidential Council, which had also been formed in September 1962 and had consisted of seven Vice-Presidents, Aly Sabry, and three other members, was abolished. Abdul Hakim Amer became First Vice-President (a new office), and Hussein el-Shafei, Hassan Ibrahim and Zakariya Muhieddin the three Vice-Presidents.

On 23 March President Nasser proclaimed the new provisional constitution, which described the United Arab Republic as a 'democratic socialist State based on the alliance of the peoples' working forces', and defined the powers of the President, the National Assembly and the Cabinet. The President has the power to appoint one or more Vice-Presidents (including a first Vice-President who would assume his powers on his death in office until a new President could be elected). He also appoints and dismisses Ministers. According to Article 113, the President 'in collaboration with the Government lays down the general policy of the State in all political, economic and social and administrative fields and supervises its execution'. He has the power to initiate, oppose and promulgate laws. If he opposes a draft law, he refers it back to the Assembly; but if the Assembly then passes it a second time by a two-thirds majority, it becomes law. If the Assembly is not in session, the President can promulgate laws by decree, but they must be referred to the Assembly within fifteen days of the opening of its next session.

The Assembly is described as the executive power of the State controlling the acts of the executive in the manner established by the constitution. Members are elected by secret universal suffrage and must be at least thirty years old. The Assembly's mandate is for five years, and a new election must take place within sixty days of its dissolution. Draft laws submitted by one or more members are transferred to an Assembly committee, which decides whether or not to refer it to the Assembly. Each article of the draft law must be voted on by the Assembly, and it only becomes law if it receives an absolute majority of those present. A quorum is a majority of the Assembly members.

No tax may be imposed, modified or abolished except by law, and the law establishes the basis for raising public funds and the manner of spending them. No loan or any major economic project may be contracted by the Treasury without the Assembly's approval.

The government is responsible to the Assembly, which will discuss its political declarations and its reports. The Assembly has the right to withdraw confidence from the government or any one of its members. Ministers may take part in the meetings of the Assembly or any of its committees whenever they wish, but they have no vote unless they are members of the Assembly. Any member of the Assembly has the right to question any Minister, who must respond. A motion of censure on the government may be introduced by ten members, and if it is adopted the government must resign. The President has the right to dissolve the Assembly, but he must call fresh elections within sixty days. A member of the Assembly has full parliamentary immunity, and he can only be deprived of his seat by a two-thirds majority of the Assembly.

In his speech at the inauguration of the Assembly, Nasser made every effort to strengthen the impression that the Egyptian

Revolution was embarking on an important new stage of development. He said that the period of transformation was over and the period of upsurge had begun. The transformation had been necessary to destroy the power of the feudalists and exploiting capitalists and change Egypt's social structure. Now that this had been done, there were three great objectives before the nation: development – doubling the national income in ten years; democracy – completing the structure of the Arab Socialist Union; and the drive towards Arab unity.

Nasser described the Assembly as a 'phenomenon of the new era'. No representative assembly in the history of Egypt's political development had ever had such an opportunity to serve the nation. He added that 'the Assembly, which is based on the will of the people, should remain with the people; it should not set itself above the people by ignoring their demands or fall below their hopes through neglect'. At another point, he said: 'True democracy cannot be achieved unless there is a powerful and effective political organization and unless there are elected people's councils to pass every decision as a free expression of the people's will.' Finally, in listing the chief problems which the country had to contend with in the new era, he included

the problem of government. We have to confess that despite all efforts it has not been developed to the point of being able to offer its services to society. It still holds itself superior to the people, assuming authority and showing reluctance to realize that it should be the servant of the masses.

The decision to democratize Egypt's highly authoritarian system of government by spreading authority downwards and outwards had been taken and repeatedly emphasized with obvious sincerity by Nasser himself. By 1964 the foundations of the country's new political organization had been laid; but by the summer of 1965 the framework was still far from complete, and it was still too soon for a fair estimate to be made of whether the structure would stand up to time and change. It would certainly be premature to condemn the project as a failure, and it is possible only to note some of the hopeful signs as well as the obstacles yet to be overcome.

THE NATIONAL ASSEMBLY

It is fair to say that this has turned out to be a more lively and independent-minded body than many people expected. Some of the members are deadwood, as in any parliament, but many of those elected for the first time in their lives have, after losing their initial shyness, made important contributions to the Assembly debates, committee discussions, and the questioning of Ministers. Furthermore, the rather crude device of reserving half the seats to 'workers and farmers' has been successful in producing a parliament which is far more representative of the Egyptian people as a whole than any of its predecessors. This is emphasized by the atmosphere and appearance of the Assembly, with the heavy sprinkling of *gallabiyahs* among the business suits.

On the other hand, the Assembly has not yet exerted anything like its full potential authority on the executive. This is largely because there are no parties or blocks and members have not yet formed groups to vote together on particular issues, although this may happen in time. When a parliamentary committee proposed a tax on refrigerators, among other things, to pay for the provision of more potable water for villages, the government objected, and by throwing his weight against the proposal, Aly Sabry was able to have the tax placed on petrol instead. In late 1964, however, the Assembly acted as a body to delay the application of the Minister of Higher Education's programme for one year pending its revision. Members opposed his proposal to lengthen the period of higher educational study in Commerce and Agriculture, and though quite possibly he had excellent reasons, there was no doubt that the voice of the people was against him.

In theory the National Assembly is a Constituent Assembly, charged with drafting a permanent constitution for the country and it will be interesting to see whether it makes any amendments to President Nasser's temporary constitution. The biggest potential difficulty, in the author's view, will be the demarcation of authority between the National Assembly, the various organs of the Arab Socialist Union, and other elected or semi-elected bodies in the State such as trade-unions and boards of directors.

In theory, the National Assembly was to be an organ of the A.S.U., but in fact its connexion with the Union is very tenuous. It is elected directly by universal suffrage, and since the distinction between active and associate members of the A.S.U. has never been applied, almost anyone was able to stand for election. Moreover, because it has been much more difficult and taken more time to build up the pyramidal framework of the A.S.U., the National Assembly met long before the National Conference of the A.S.U., which is supposed to lay down the broad principles of the country's policies. By the time the Conference, which will include representatives from all the basic units in the country, does meet, the Assembly will have the bit between its teeth and is unlikely to welcome directives from anyone.

Ultimately it is intended that the National Conference should elect its own General Council, which in turn will elect a twenty-five-member Higher Executive Committee. The Higher Executive Committee which was appointed by the President to direct and supervise the creation of the whole A.S.U. organization is therefore in theory only a temporary body, which will be replaced by the new elected committee. In fact this temporary Higher Executive, which includes all the Vice-Presidents, the Prime Minister and Deputy Prime Ministers, has been acting as the successor to the Presidential Council. The real test for the A.S.U. will come when the National Conference has to elect its own Higher Executive, and it will be interesting to see whether it has the courage to replace some of the President's appointees with men of its own choice.

In all public companies, firms, or organizations, there are now likely to be three different categories of men elected by the workers and employees to represent them – the twenty-man committee of the A.S.U. basic unit, trade-union officials, and the four members elected to the board of directors (two of whom are normally workers and two salaried employees). Clearly this may raise a serious clash of interests and loyalties. At present the management finds the trade-unionists more mature and reasonable to deal with than the A.S.U. committees, but this may only be an indication that the trade-unions are out of touch with the real feelings of the workers. The trade-unions are, after all, virtually a branch of the government. It is not improbable that in time the A.S.U. will become the means by which the workers express their real grievances. This might be inconvenient for the government, but it would give the A.S.U. vitality.

At the higher level it is proposed to set up specialized A.S.U. committees for such matters as Housing, Labour, Social Affairs and Higher Education, to supervise the work of the Ministries. The idea of having such ginger groups to prod and stimulate sluggish civil servants may be excellent, but the Ministries are unlikely to accept such interference with a good grace.

All these difficulties have been raised and discussed in the Press, but they can hardly be overcome until Egypt's new political organization is complete and can be tested in practice. As always, Nasser's approach is pragmatic. If something does not work, he discards it and tries to think again. But the important thing is that it is still he who does most of the thinking; the A.S.U. organization is almost entirely his own idea. The real test must be whether the Union can develop a life of its own, for if it becomes merely an elaborate system for rubber-stamping the government's policies, the public will lose interest, and it will wither away. Significantly Nasser has staked heavily on making it work. He has devoted thought and effort to it as he never did to the National Union or the Liberation Rally, and if it fails, it is hard to see what he could turn to next.

On 18, 19 and 20 January 1965, the streets of Cairo were filled with processions of Egyptians converging on the National Assembly. *Fellahin* who had come by train from the country, nurses, schoolchildren and workers who had been given the day off for the purpose were demanding Gamal Abdul Nasser's nomination for another six-year term as president. When the vote was finally taken on the evening of 20 January, there were several hundred thousand people jammed into the streets surrounding the National Assembly. The voting was 355 in favour out of 360. Two were absent, and the remaining three who abstained were never identified.

This extraordinary demonstration in favour of what was after all a foregone conclusion showed both the strength and weakness of Egypt's present political situation. No one who saw it can have felt that it was a regimented affair organized by a ruthless totalitarian State. The noisy laughing demonstrators, sometimes led by an enthusiastic amateur band, were clearly having a good time. But they were also an expression of the undeniable fact that despite the grumbles and the anarchic cynical jokes about the regime, the vast majority of the Egyptian people want Abdul Nasser to remain as their leader and would be appalled if anything happened to him. In spite of his youth, he is a loved and trusted father figure. If he had not categorically refused on several occasions, they would have made him president for life.

The advantage to Egypt of this loyalty and affection for its leader has been its extraordinary stability over the past twelve eventful years, which have seen a revolutionary change in its own society and its relations with the outside world. The weakness lies in the frightening dependence on a single human being. Nasser himself is genuinely anxious to reduce this dependence and to spread his load of responsibility through a more democratic political system; but he has so far been prevented, partly by his own character and personality, and partly by the nature of the Egyptian people themselves.

It should not be forgotten that Nasser rose to power not as the leader of a political party or mass independence movement, but as the brilliantly successful organizer of a *coup* by young army officers. He inspired confidence and admiration in the small circle of those who knew him well, but he had no public personality at all. In time he showed that he had the qualities of charismatic leadership, but these were not obvious for some years after the Revolution. In the early days the attitude of the public towards him was suspicious and slightly hostile. His speeches were heard politely but without enthusiasm, and it was only with time and some difficulty that he developed a style of oratory which reached the people's hearts (the breakthrough is generally thought to have been made with his Alexandria speech in July 1956, when he announced the nationalization of the Suez Canal).

Even today he is far from being an instinctive politician in the sense that the Western democracies know. Although he has intense personal charm in private conversation which sometimes captivates the most hostile (to their own alarm and dismay), he remains somewhat remote and reserved, as if he were keeping back the major part of his thoughts. Those who have watched him on official social occasions have noted that he only appears to be on easy intimate terms with two men – Abdul Hakim Amer and Muhammad Hasanein Heykal. All the other senior members of the regime stand too much in awe of him to have this kind of relationship.

Another aspect of this is that no other member of the regime has developed a public personality. Some of them are of high intelligence and ability. Amer is a popular and respected army commander; Aly Sabry is acknowledged to be a good hard-working administrator; Dr Kaissouny is a first-class Finance Minister; and Dr Hatem has disproved the popular notion that no Egyptian Minister is capable of working very hard for long hours. But as individuals they are virtually unknown to the public, and it is significant that Cairo's talented corps of caricaturists has been unable to make anything out of them. If they have any difference of opinion, only the faintest whisper of it reaches the outside world. When the government was reformed in March 1963, two striking omissions from high office of any kind were Abdul Latif el-Baghdadi and Kamal el-din Hussein. Several theories were put forward to explain Baghdadi's absence: one, that he was in very poor health; and another, that he did not feel he could accept any office except that of First Vice-President, which had already been given to Amer. It was widely believed that Kamal el-din Hussein had disagreed with Egypt's involvement in Yemen. But in neither case was there the slightest official hint of the reason, and the Press did not discuss it. The public was left to guess.

This secretiveness is characteristic of all Egypt's public life today. It is partly because Nasser and his chief associates are ex-army officers. Although Nasser himself very wisely insisted from an early date after the Revolution that the officers should civilian-ize themselves and drop their military ranks (so that it is quite incorrect to continue referring to 'Colonel Nasser' or 'Colonel Hatem', as some Western journals insist on doing), they have never dropped the military view that orders are to be obeyed by subordinates without discussion. In the past twelve years there have been many times when this attitude has been an advantage. In the series of external crises in which Egypt has been involved, firm and rapid decision at the top has been essential, while today the country's massive frontal attack on poverty and ignorance, requiring the mobilization of all its human and material resources, bears all the characteristics of a military operation. But it is not 'true democracy' of the kind that Nasser has quite genuinely declared that he wants to see in Egypt. For this the people will at least have to be allowed to inform themselves on a whole range of State matters, especially foreign policy, which at present are kept secret.

If Egypt's regime is excessively authoritarian, it is only partly the fault of those at the top; it is also the consequence of the last two thousand years of history which have made the people submissive to authority. The Egyptians are not natural rebels or martyrs. There is an elaborate secret police apparatus which is widely believed to tap the telephone and watch the activities of all resident foreigners and prominent Egyptians in sensitive positions. If this police force did everything that it is said to do, it would have to be at least ten million strong, but it is undeniably widespread and active. Like the intelligence services of other countries, it often seems to act independently of the government's authority, yet it does not bear comparison with the cold-blooded ruthlessness of most modern totalitarian States. It is less efficient and more human. This is not to belittle the sufferings of political prisoners who spent many years in camps and prisons and a few of whom died from ill-treatment. Most of these were either Muslim Brothers or Communists preaching a revolution that would have been much more violent than the one Egypt has passed through since 1952, but some of those imprisoned as Communists were highly theoretical left-wing intellectuals who hardly threatened the State. They have now, however, all been released and the prison camps closed. Some of the Marxist intellectuals who are reconciled with the regime have been reinstated with the Press. In *al-Tali'ah* (Vanguard), a political monthly magazine which *al-Ahram* began to publish in

January 1965, a group of them are making an interesting effort to develop a synthesis of Marxism and the ideas in the National Charter.

The choice of *al-Tali'ah* as a title is significant. So far from forming the vanguard of the revolutionary movement in Egypt, the intellectuals took no part in it. They were subsequently cold-shouldered by the regime and for the most part retired to sulk. There was some justice in their claim that the young officers were only interested in the technology of the West and not in its culture and ideas – whether traditional or Marxist – whereas what Egypt needs more than an industrial–technical revolution is the intellectual revolution which it missed in the eighteenth and nineteenth centuries. It could equally be said that Egypt's intellectual élite had already opted out of the struggle before July 1952. It is little use trying to lead an intellectual revolution in your own country without a profound knowledge and under-standing of it, and this is what all but a sprinkling of Egyptian intellectuals lacked. As Father Ayrout remarked in his *Fellah* (published before 1952):

The élite turns away from the masses; it has kept for itself, for politics, literature or for Europe its intelligence, its civilization, its culture and its money. It has lacked devotion or, as some would say, patriotism.

The reconciliation between the intellectuals and the regime, of which there are signs, could benefit both sides. But it is doubt-ful whether Nasser himself really expects the intellectuals to assume the vanguard position. Everything he has said or written points to a belief that Egypt's future leaders are among the *fella-hin* and the workers (ex-*fellahin*). As the French archaeologist remarks in a novel *The Rediscovered Soul* by Tawfik el-Hakim, Nasser's favourite Egyptian author:

Europe has failed to understand that these people whom we regard as ignorant know many things. The Great Wisdom flows in his blood but it flows without his knowledge. . . . Can you really believe that the thousands of years which make up Egypt's past have vanished like a dream without a trace?

This idea that the descendants of the men who built the pyramids will once again astonish the world is fundamental to Nasser's thinking. But he is also aware of the extreme difficulty of reviving a spirit which has been buried under thousands of years of history. As he said at the opening of the National Assembly in 1957:

We must always keep in mind that the most important, the most difficult, the most crucial of our problems is to create in this part of the world a dynamic and watchful nation and that human beings are the raw material from which a nation is made. Therefore to build a new Egypt our effort must be concentrated on the rational development of the latent potential that our Creator has given to this raw material.

To build factories is easy, to build hospitals and schools is possible, but to build a nation of men is a hard and difficult task.

Maxime du Camp, the French writer who visited Egypt with Gustave Flaubert in 1849, wrote: 'The old race – copts and *fellahin* – lives as it used to live, humiliated, exploited by the conqueror . . . the Egyptian seems created to obey, because whoever rules him he obeys.' Until recently this was the accepted view of Egypt, and the fact that Gamal Abdul Nasser has upset it accounts for the hostility he arouses in the outside world, a hostility which far exceeds anything provoked by Ben Bella, Sukarno or other dynamic nationalist leaders of under-developed nations. But it is essentially Nasser who has forced the world to reassess Egypt and not the Egyptians themselves. We know from the *Philosophy of the Revolution* that he foresaw with extraordinary clarity from the earliest days of the Revolution, and perhaps before, the role that Egypt's strategic position gave it the chance to play in the world provided it could find a leader. Aided by a few devoted lieutenants, he has succeeded in hauling the Egyptian people on to the world stage by the scruff of their necks to play the role. Most of them still suffer from stage fright.

As with all human blueprints, things have not worked out exactly as he thought. Of the three famous circles which he saw converging in Cairo, the Arab one has turned out to be much the most important to Egypt, followed by the African and finally the Islamic. Islam is an immensely important element in both Arab nationalism and Nasser's outlook, but pan-Islam, in the sense of the unity of all the predominantly Muslim countries, is not. Some of the young officers toyed with the idea in the early days of the Revolution, but they soon dropped it. The author has sometimes been told by Indians that they fear the formation of an Islamic front of the Arab States, Pakistan, Iran and the South-East Asian Muslim countries, which could encircle secular India. All one can say is that there is very little sign of this happening at present. Since the Revolution, Egypt has judged nations by their political attitudes rather than their religion, which is why it has always been closer to non-aligned socialist India than to the pro-Western Muslim members of CENTO – Pakistan, Iran and Turkey. It is true that in Africa, Egypt finds it slightly easier to extend its contacts with the Islamic States south of the Sahara than the non-Islamic. But this is largely because the Muslims have more sympathy for the Arab attitude to Israel. In the last resort Nasser will feel closer to a radical socialist Nkrumah than to a conservative if Muslim Prime Minister of Nigeria.

What Nasser probably did not see at the time of the Revolution was the extent to which Egypt's influence abroad would depend on its domestic policies. Between 1955 and 1965 Egypt was a pace-setter for social and economic change in the Arab world and even beyond in Africa. In every one of these countries where feudal aristocracies have begun to use their incomes to build schools and hospitals rather than palaces, the pressure of Egypt's example, loudly publicized by Cairo radio, has had something to do with it.

But having set the pace, Egypt has to show that it can arrive. Under Nasser, Egypt has already proved that it is possible for a small weak nation with few resources to act as an autonomous power in defiance of old imperial or neo-colonial influences. But it also has to show that it can emerge from social and economic backwardness to the status of a developed nation. If it does, the Egyptian 1952 Revolution will be a seminal event of the twentieth century. If it does not, Nasserism will leave as little impression on the world as Italian fascism.

Index

Index

Index

Index

Index

More About Penguins

If you have enjoyed reading this book you may wish
to know that *Penguin Book News* appears every month.
It is an attractively illustrated magazine containing
a complete list of books published by Penguins and
still in print, together with details of the month's
new books. A specimen copy will be sent free on
request.

Penguin Book News is obtainable from most bookshops;
but you may prefer to become a regular subscriber at
3s. for twelve issues. Just write to Dept EP, Penguin
Books Ltd, Harmondsworth, Middlesex, enclosing
a cheque or postal order, and you will be put on the
mailing list.

Another book in the Penguin African Library
is described overleaf.

Note: *Penguin Book News* is not available in the U.S.A.

WHICH WAY AFRICA?

The Search for a New Society

Basil Davidson

A man would have to be very brave or very foolhardy to try to forecast precisely the pattern of Africa's future. Where events outrun the printing-presses, discretion is the better part of omniscience.

In *Which Way Africa?* Basil Davidson, the well-known writer on African affairs, has steered clear of political ju-ju. Instead – and infinitely more to the purpose – he has made what is the only up-to-date and comprehensive analysis in English – and probably in any language – of the social, economic, and political motives, myths, ideas and beliefs which underly modern African nationalism.

Events in Tanganyika, Zanzibar, the Congo and Ghana have shown the world an Africa poised on the threshold of new ventures, an Africa in flux. Only such an analysis as the author has successfully achieved in this volume can help to delineate the kind of societies which will now tend to emerge there.